THE ROAD TO HELL

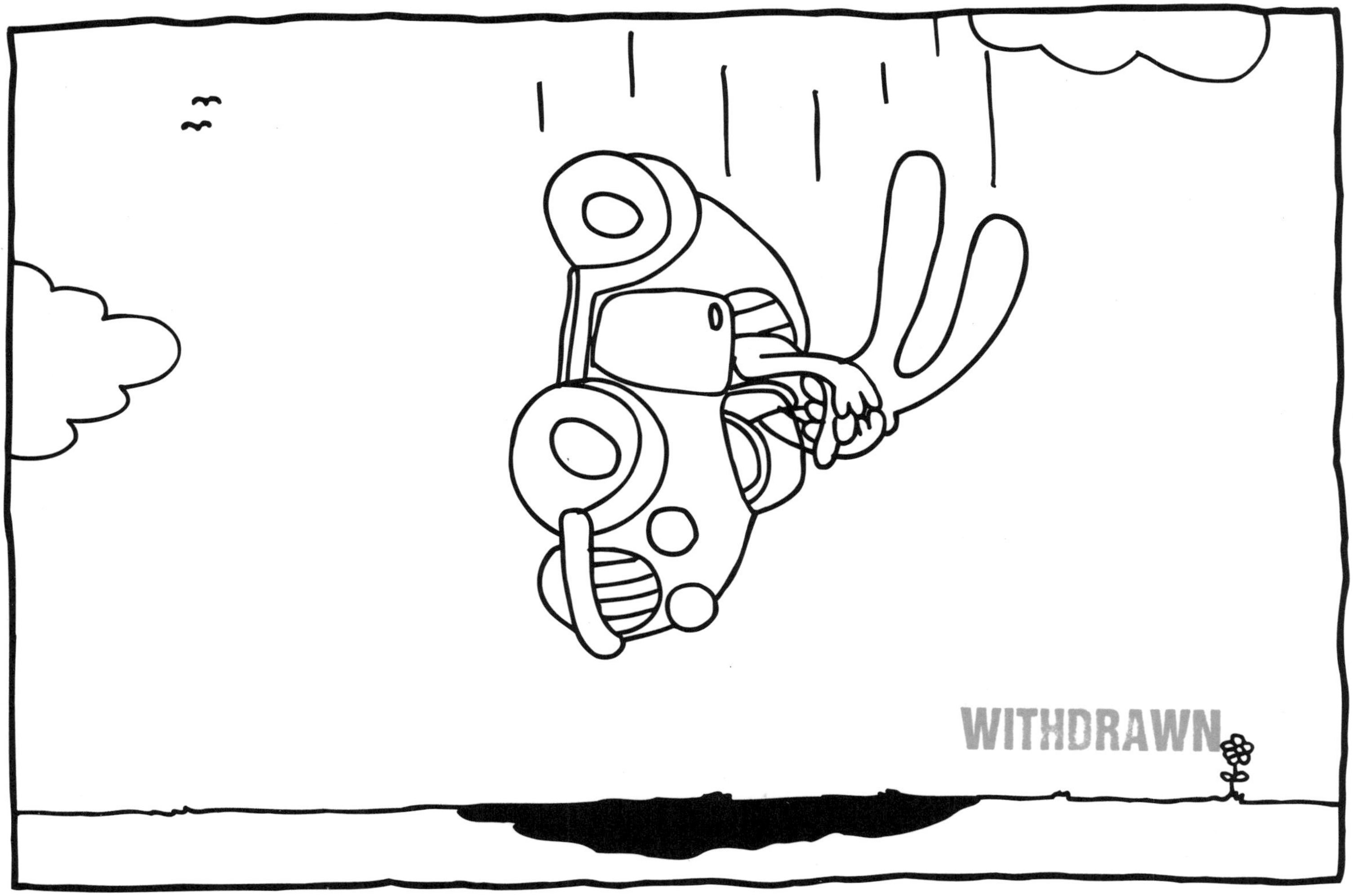

A CARTOON BOOK BY MATT GROENING

OTHER BOOKS BY THIS CARTOONIST HIMSELF

LOVE IS HELL
WORK IS HELL
SCHOOL IS HELL
CHILDHOOD IS HELL
AKBAR & JEFF'S GUIDE TO LIFE
THE BIG BOOK OF HELL
HOW TO GO TO HELL

WORKS IN PROGRESS

THE SHOCKING TRUTH ABOUT AKBAR (BY JEFF)
THE SHOCKING AND REVOLTING TRUTH ABOUT JEFF (BY AKBAR)
THAT DEVIOUS LITTLE SNEAK, AKBAR (BY JEFF)
JEFF: THE BIGGEST LIAR OF THEM ALL (BY AKBAR)
THE MAYBE-WE-SHOULD-FORGIVE-EACH-OTHER BOOK (BY JEFF)
THE I-LOVE-YOU-FOREVER BOOK (BY AKBAR)
AKBAR & JEFF'S BIG BOOK OF LINGERING RESENTMENTS

FIRST EDITION

COVER DESIGN: MILI SMYTHE
LEGAL COUNSEL: SUSAN GRODE
EDITOR: WENDY WOLF
SPECIAL THANKS TO: SONDRA ROBINSON, JEANNINE CROWELL, EILEEN CAMPION, AND THE RADIANT DEBORAH CAPLAN

DEDICATED TO STEVE AND CINDY VANCE, DESIGN AND DIVING BUDDIES.

LYNDA BARRY PLAYS FUNKY ACCORDION.

ISBN 0-06-096950-4

92 93 94 95 96 RRD 10 9 8 7 6 5 4 3 2

HarperPerennial
A Division of HarperCollinsPublishers

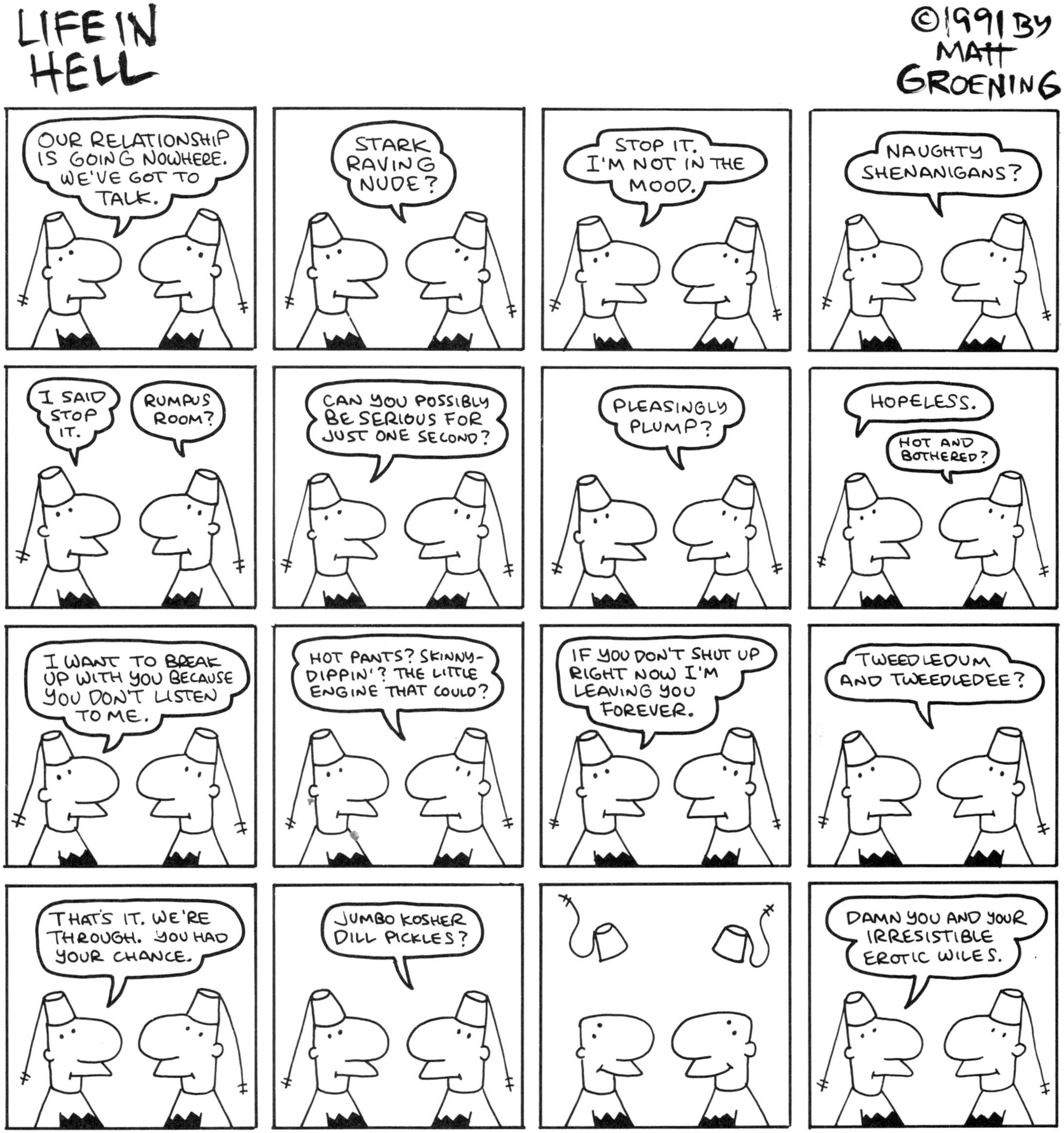
LIFE IN HELL
©1991 BY MATT GROENING
OUR RELATIONSHIP IS GOING NOWHERE. WE'VE GOT TO TALK.
STARK RAVING NUDE?
STOP IT. I'M NOT IN THE MOOD.
NAUGHTY SHENANIGANS?
I SAID STOP IT.
RUMPUS ROOM?
CAN YOU POSSIBLY BE SERIOUS FOR JUST ONE SECOND?
PLEASINGLY PLUMP?
HOPELESS.
HOT AND BOTHERED?
I WANT TO BREAK UP WITH YOU BECAUSE YOU DON'T LISTEN TO ME.
HOT PANTS? SKINNY-DIPPIN'? THE LITTLE ENGINE THAT COULD?
IF YOU DON'T SHUT UP RIGHT NOW I'M LEAVING YOU FOREVER.
TWEEDLEDUM AND TWEEDLEDEE?
THAT'S IT. WE'RE THROUGH. YOU HAD YOUR CHANCE.
JUMBO KOSHER DILL PICKLES?
DAMN YOU AND YOUR IRRESISTIBLE EROTIC WILES.

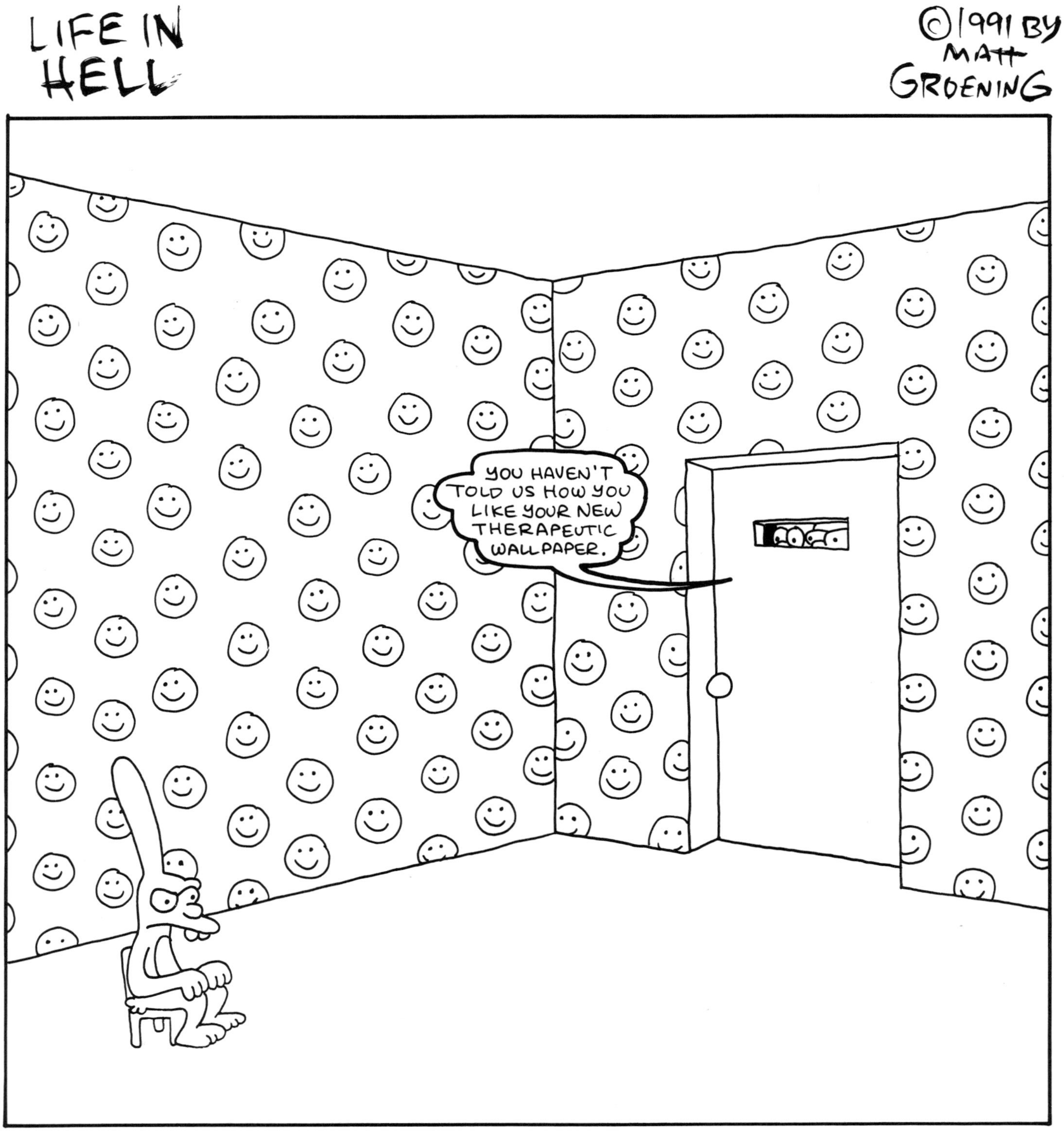
LIFE IN HELL
©1991 BY MATT GROENING
YOU HAVEN'T TOLD US HOW YOU LIKE YOUR NEW THERAPEUTIC WALLPAPER.

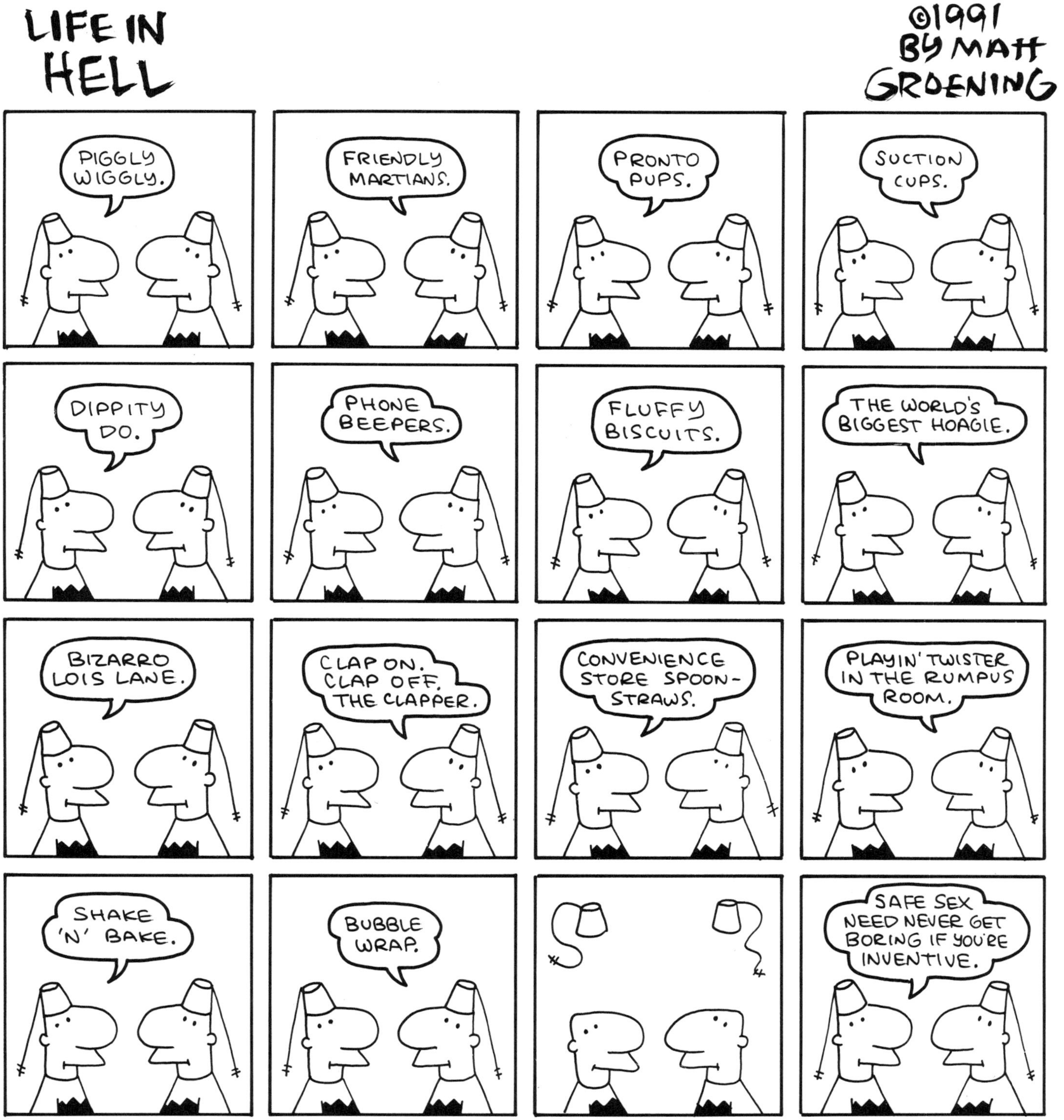
LIFE IN HELL
©1991 BY MATT GROENING
PIGGLY WIGGLY.
FRIENDLY MARTIANS.
PRONTO PUPS.
SUCTION CUPS.
DIPPITY DO.
PHONE BEEPERS.
FLUFFY BISCUITS.
THE WORLD'S BIGGEST HOAGIE.
BIZARRO LOIS LANE.
CLAP ON. CLAP OFF. THE CLAPPER.
CONVENIENCE STORE SPOON-STRAWS.
PLAYIN' TWISTER IN THE RUMPUS ROOM.
SHAKE 'N' BAKE.
BUBBLE WRAP.
SAFE SEX NEED NEVER GET BORING IF YOU'RE INVENTIVE.

LIFE IN HELL

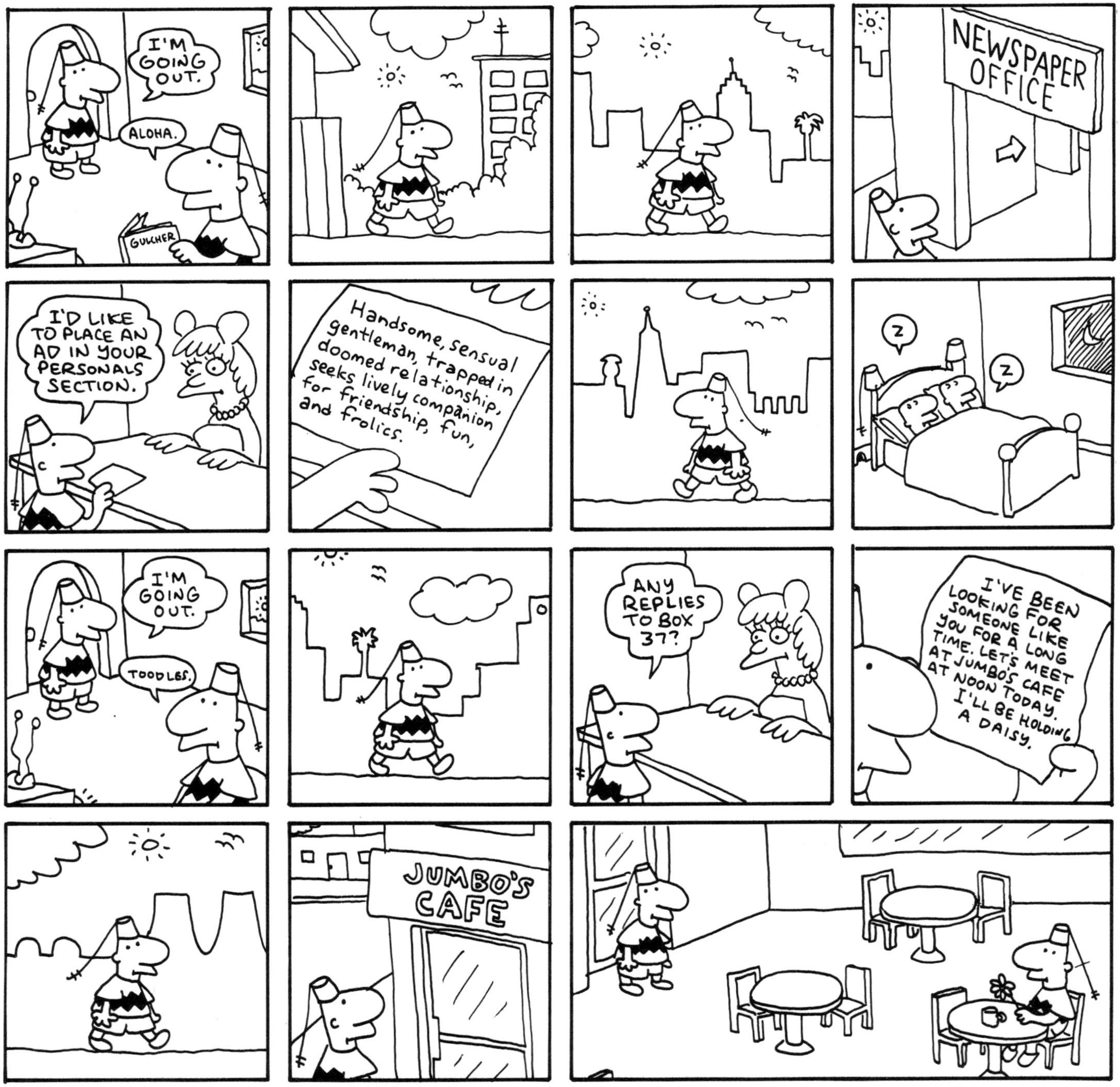

I'M GOING OUT.
ALOHA.
GULCHER
NEWSPAPER OFFICE
I'D LIKE TO PLACE AN AD IN YOUR PERSONALS SECTION.
Handsome, sensual gentleman, trapped in doomed relationship, seeks lively companion for friendship, fun, and frolics.
Z
Z
I'M GOING OUT.
TOODLES.
ANY REPLIES TO BOX 37?
I'VE BEEN LOOKING FOR SOMEONE LIKE YOU FOR A LONG TIME. LET'S MEET AT JUMBO'S CAFE AT NOON TODAY. I'LL BE HOLDING A DAISY.
JUMBO'S CAFE

LIFE IN HELL

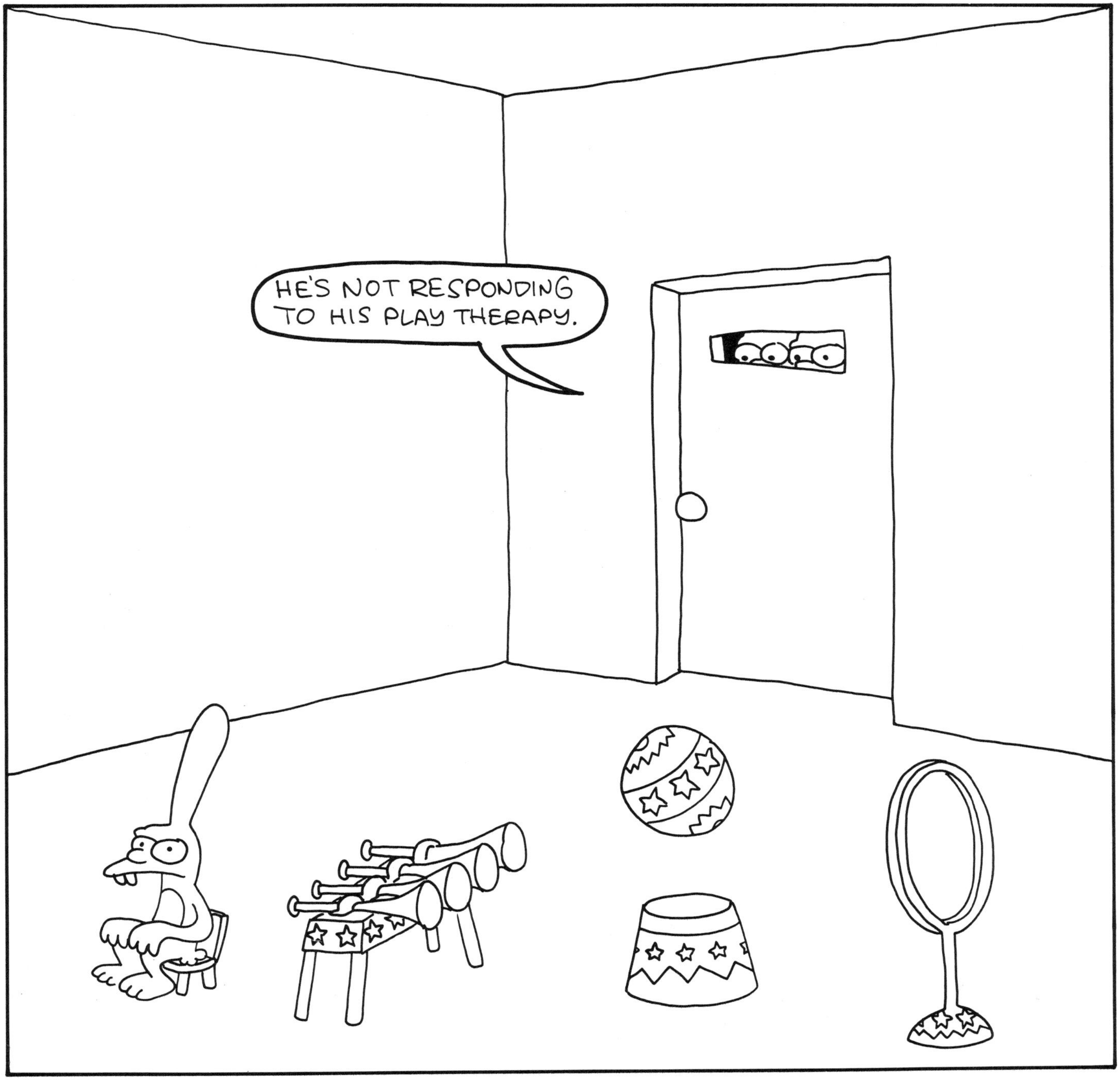
HE'S NOT RESPONDING TO HIS PLAY THERAPY.

LIFE IN HELL

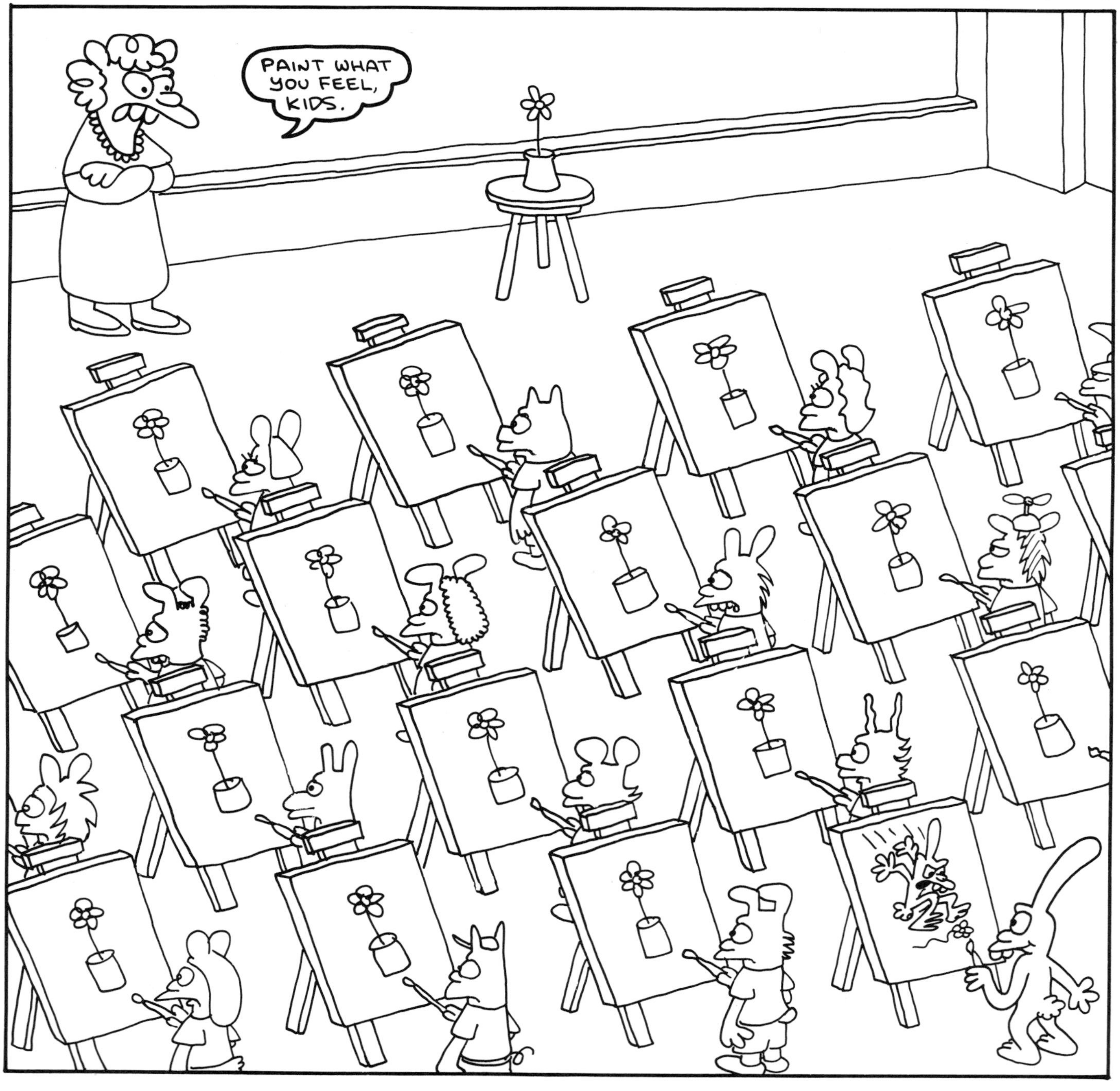
PAINT WHAT YOU FEEL, KIDS.

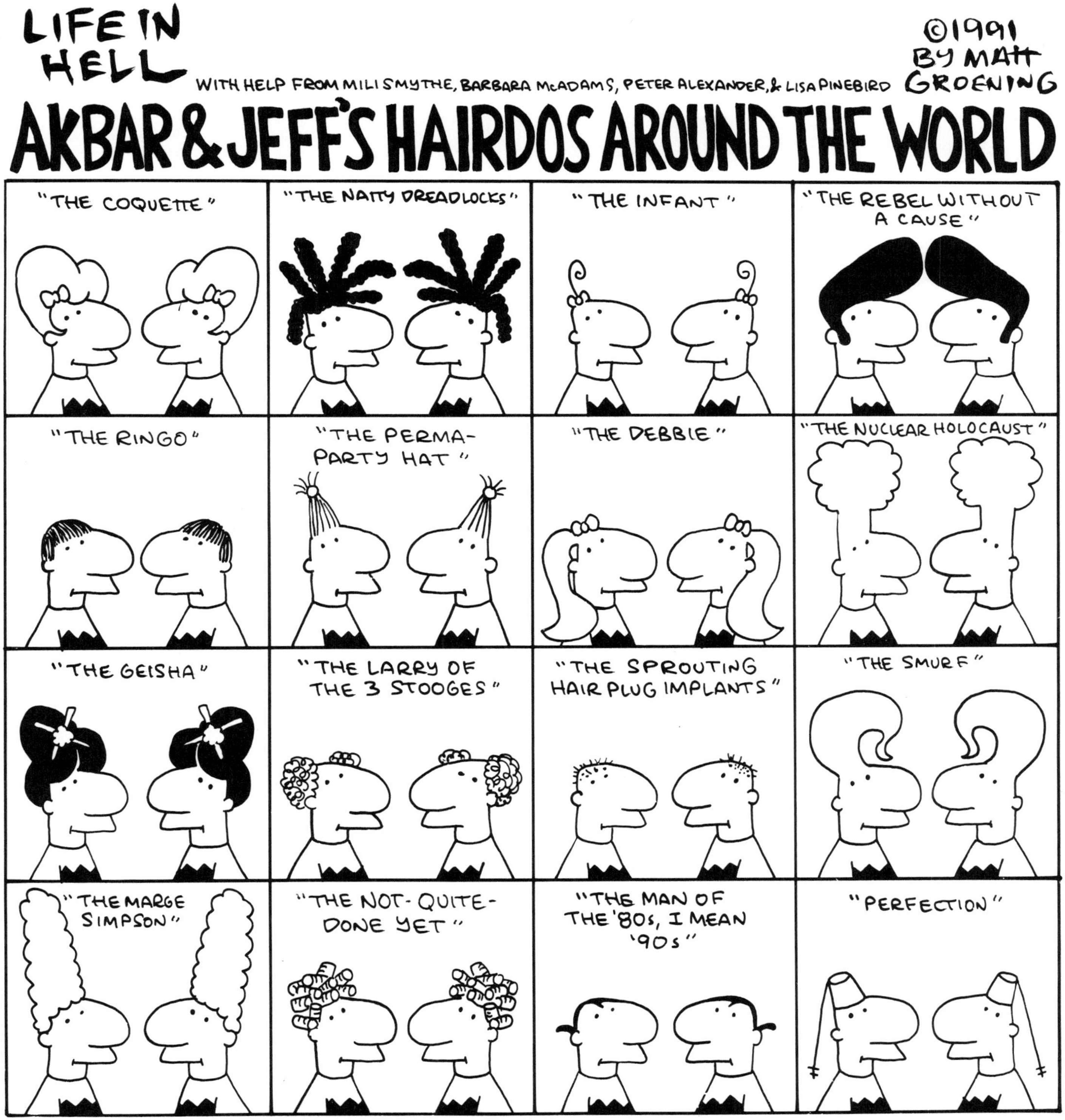
LIFE IN HELL
©1991 BY MATT GROENING
WITH HELP FROM MILI SMYTHE, BARBARA McADAMS, PETER ALEXANDER, & LISA PINEBIRD
AKBAR & JEFF'S HAIRDOS AROUND THE WORLD
"THE COQUETTE"
"THE NATTY DREADLOCKS"
"THE INFANT"
"THE REBEL WITHOUT A CAUSE"
"THE RINGO"
"THE PERMA-PARTY HAT"
"THE DEBBIE"
"THE NUCLEAR HOLOCAUST"
"THE GEISHA"
"THE LARRY OF THE 3 STOOGES"
"THE SPROUTING HAIR PLUG IMPLANTS"
"THE SMURF"
"THE MARGE SIMPSON"
"THE NOT-QUITE-DONE YET"
"THE MAN OF THE '80s, I MEAN '90s"
"PERFECTION"

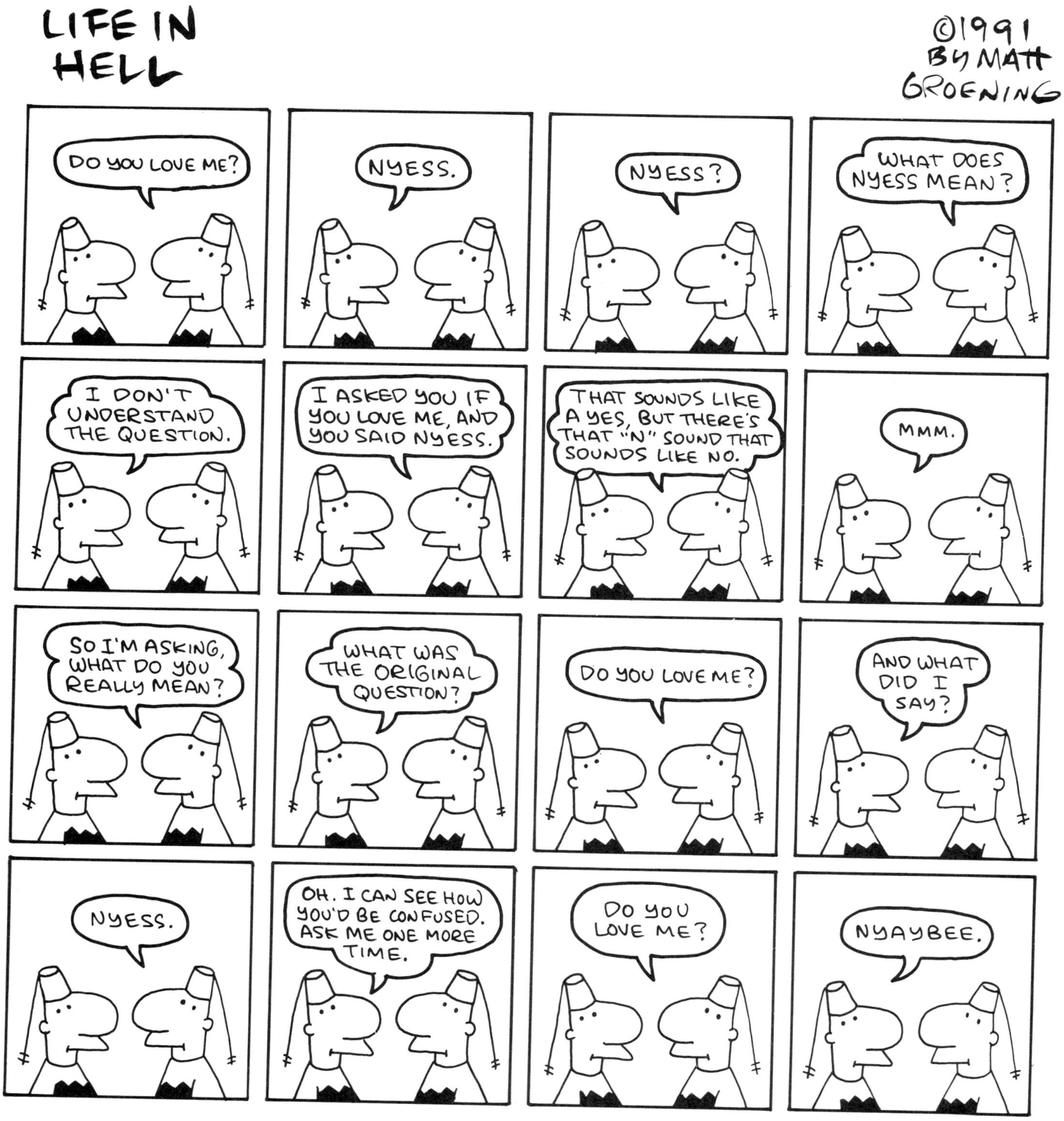

LIFE IN HELL
©1991 BY MATT GROENING
DO YOU LOVE ME?
NYESS.
NYESS?
WHAT DOES NYESS MEAN?
I DON'T UNDERSTAND THE QUESTION.
I ASKED YOU IF YOU LOVE ME, AND YOU SAID NYESS.
THAT SOUNDS LIKE A YES, BUT THERE'S THAT "N" SOUND THAT SOUNDS LIKE NO.
MMM.
SO I'M ASKING, WHAT DO YOU REALLY MEAN?
WHAT WAS THE ORIGINAL QUESTION?
DO YOU LOVE ME?
AND WHAT DID I SAY?
NYESS.
OH. I CAN SEE HOW YOU'D BE CONFUSED. ASK ME ONE MORE TIME.
DO YOU LOVE ME?
NYAYBEE.

LIFE IN HELL

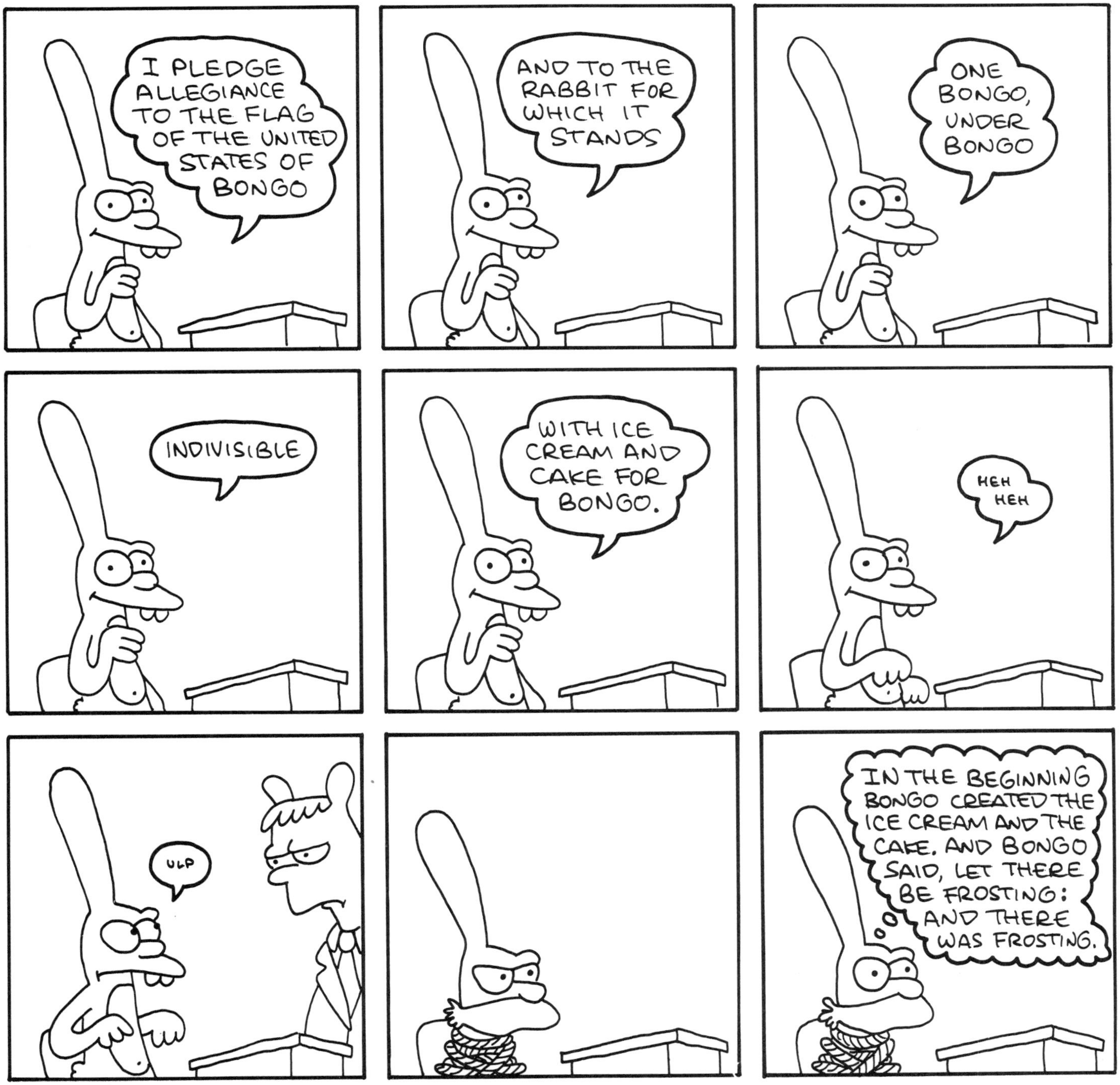
I PLEDGE ALLEGIANCE TO THE FLAG OF THE UNITED STATES OF BONGO
AND TO THE RABBIT FOR WHICH IT STANDS
ONE BONGO, UNDER BONGO
INDIVISIBLE
WITH ICE CREAM AND CAKE FOR BONGO.
HEH HEH
ULP
IN THE BEGINNING BONGO CREATED THE ICE CREAM AND THE CAKE. AND BONGO SAID, LET THERE BE FROSTING: AND THERE WAS FROSTING.

LIFE IN HELL

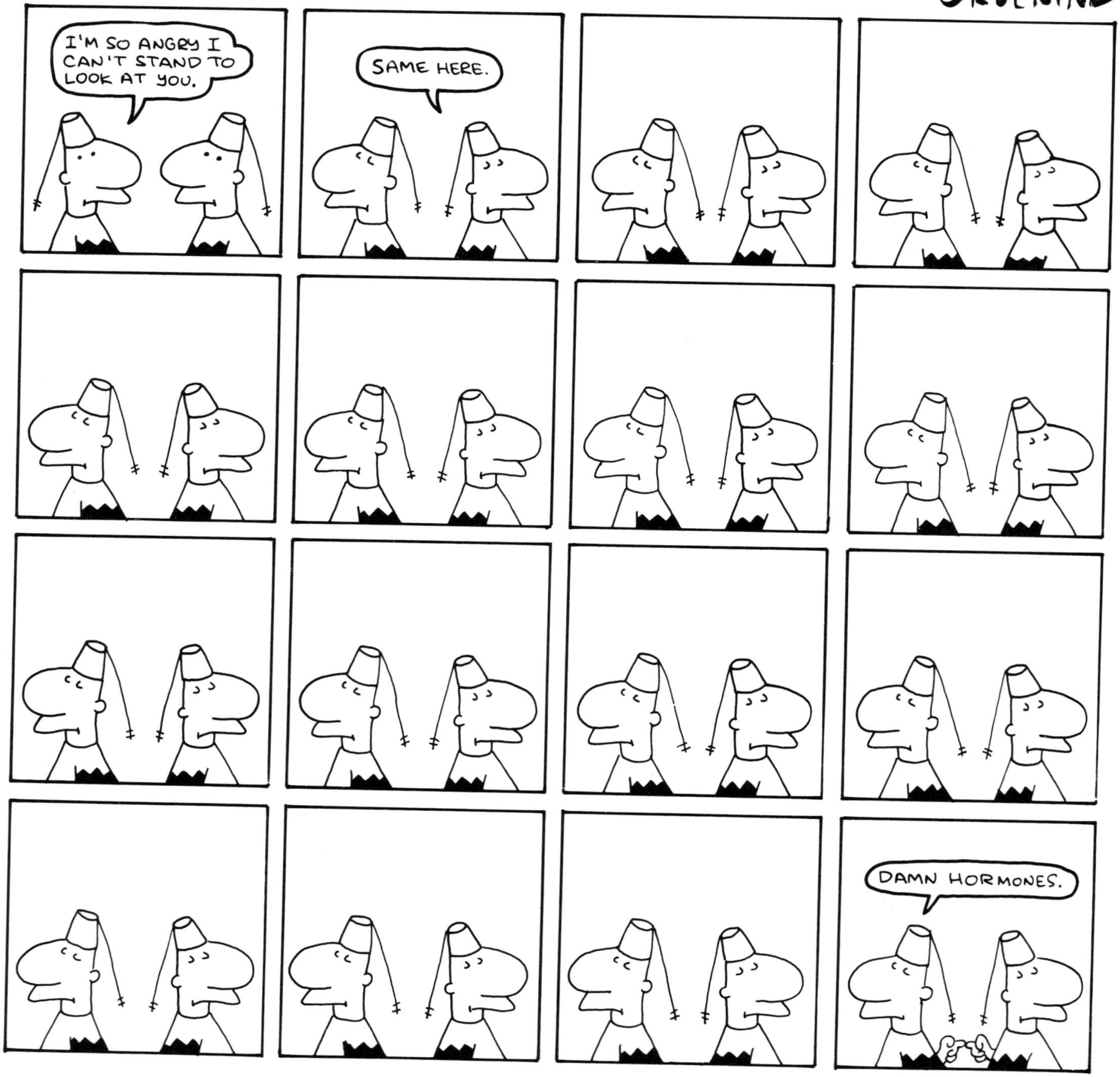
I'M SO ANGRY I CAN'T STAND TO LOOK AT YOU.
SAME HERE.
DAMN HORMONES.

LIFE IN HELL

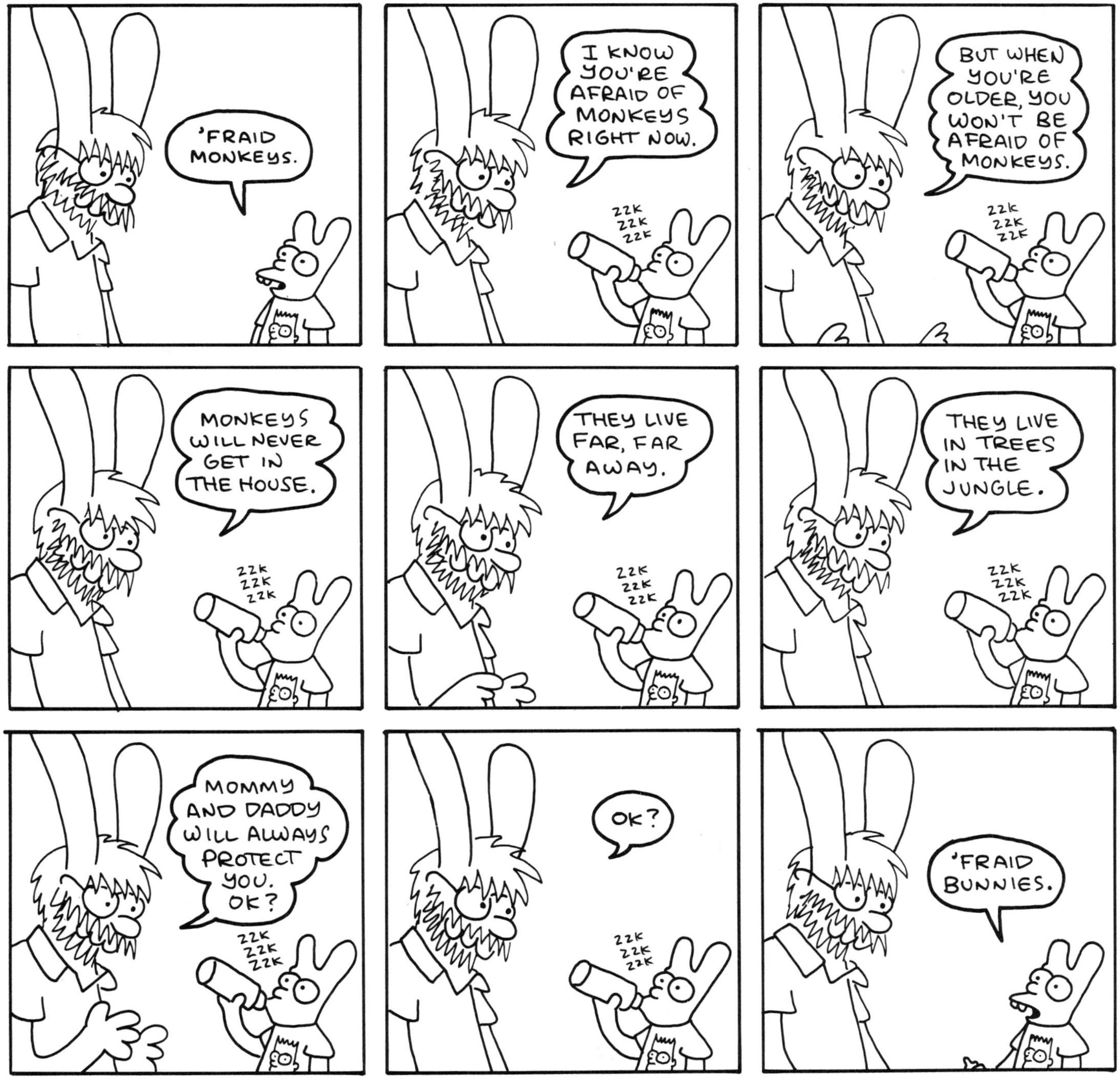
'FRAID MONKEYS.
I KNOW YOU'RE AFRAID OF MONKEYS RIGHT NOW.
ZZK ZZK ZZK
BUT WHEN YOU'RE OLDER, YOU WON'T BE AFRAID OF MONKEYS.
ZZK ZZK ZZK
MONKEYS WILL NEVER GET IN THE HOUSE.
ZZK ZZK ZZK
THEY LIVE FAR, FAR AWAY.
ZZK ZZK ZZK
THEY LIVE IN TREES IN THE JUNGLE.
ZZK ZZK ZZK
MOMMY AND DADDY WILL ALWAYS PROTECT YOU. OK?
ZZK ZZK ZZK
OK?
ZZK ZZK ZZK
'FRAID BUNNIES.

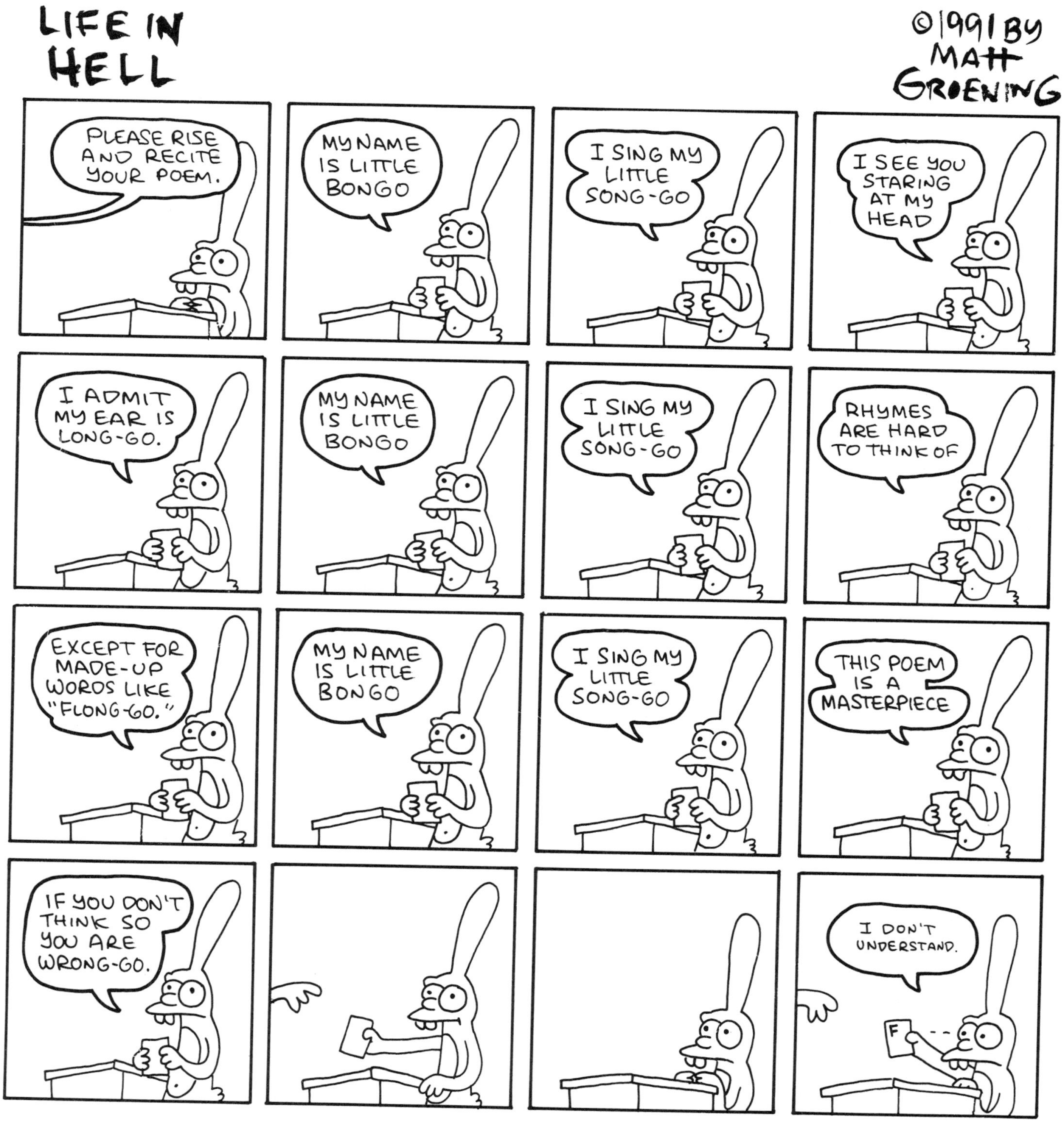
LIFE IN HELL
©1991 BY MATT GROENING
PLEASE RISE AND RECITE YOUR POEM.
MY NAME IS LITTLE BONGO
I SING MY LITTLE SONG-GO
I SEE YOU STARING AT MY HEAD
I ADMIT MY EAR IS LONG-GO.
MY NAME IS LITTLE BONGO
I SING MY LITTLE SONG-GO
RHYMES ARE HARD TO THINK OF
EXCEPT FOR MADE-UP WORDS LIKE "FLONG-GO."
MY NAME IS LITTLE BONGO
I SING MY LITTLE SONG-GO
THIS POEM IS A MASTERPIECE
IF YOU DON'T THINK SO YOU ARE WRONG-GO.
F
I DON'T UNDERSTAND.

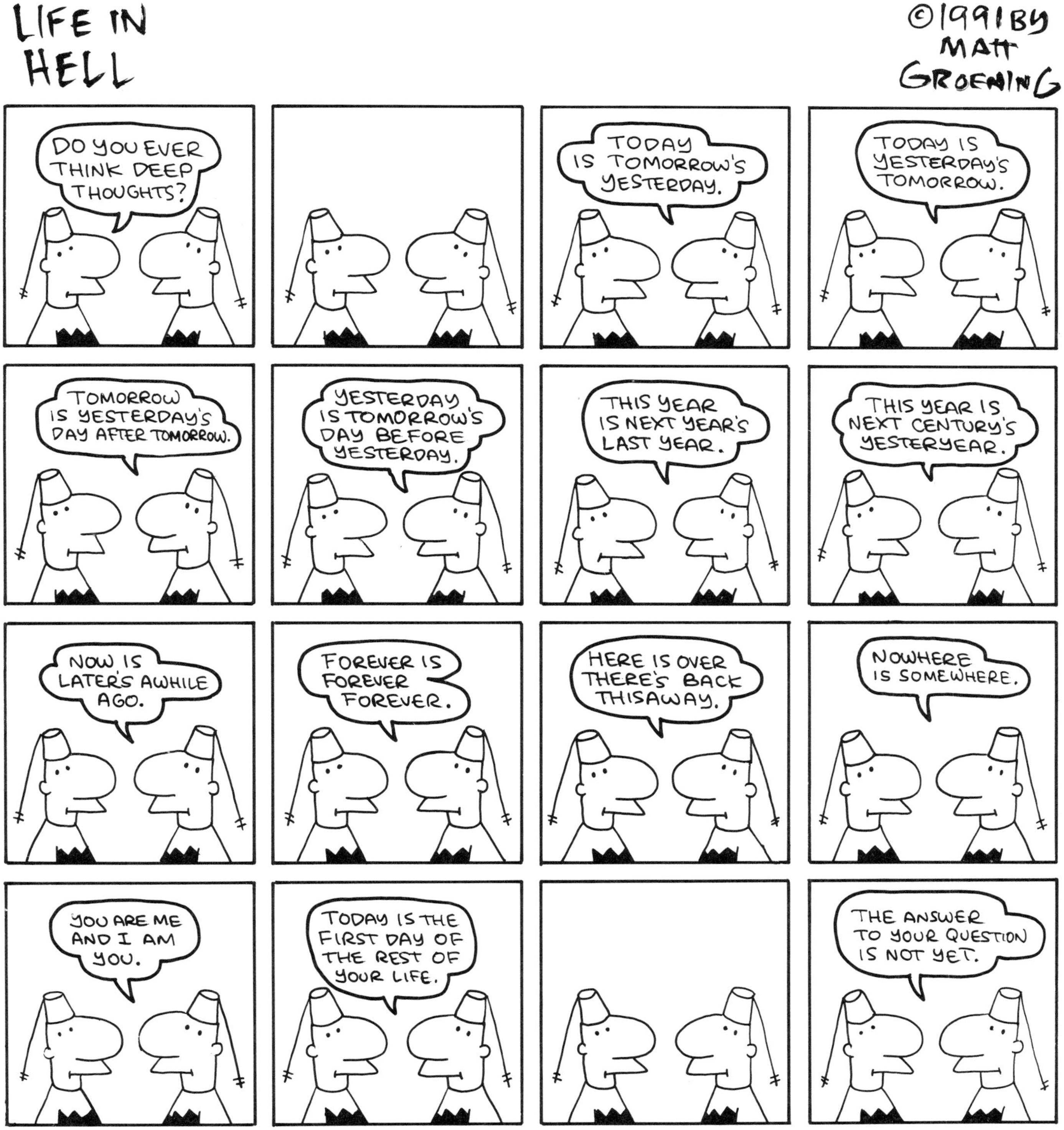
LIFE IN HELL
©1991 BY MATT GROENING
DO YOU EVER THINK DEEP THOUGHTS?
TODAY IS TOMORROW'S YESTERDAY.
TODAY IS YESTERDAY'S TOMORROW.
TOMORROW IS YESTERDAY'S DAY AFTER TOMORROW.
YESTERDAY IS TOMORROW'S DAY BEFORE YESTERDAY.
THIS YEAR IS NEXT YEAR'S LAST YEAR.
THIS YEAR IS NEXT CENTURY'S YESTERYEAR.
NOW IS LATER'S AWHILE AGO.
FOREVER IS FOREVER FOREVER.
HERE IS OVER THERE'S BACK THISAWAY.
NOWHERE IS SOMEWHERE.
YOU ARE ME AND I AM YOU.
TODAY IS THE FIRST DAY OF THE REST OF YOUR LIFE.
THE ANSWER TO YOUR QUESTION IS NOT YET.

LIFE IN HELL

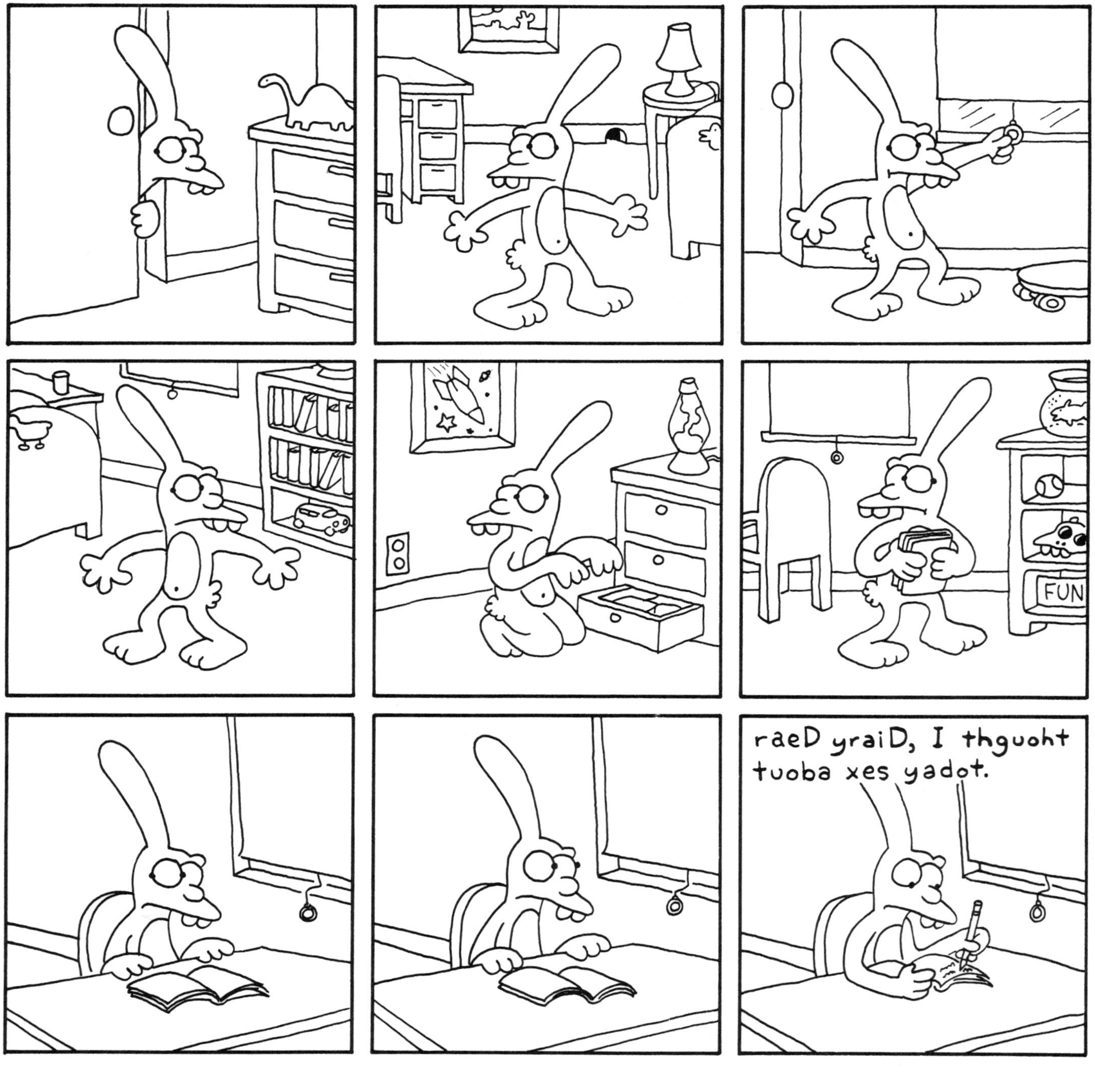
FUN
raeD yraiD, I thguoht tuoba xes yadot.

LIFE IN HELL

©1992 BY MATT GROENING

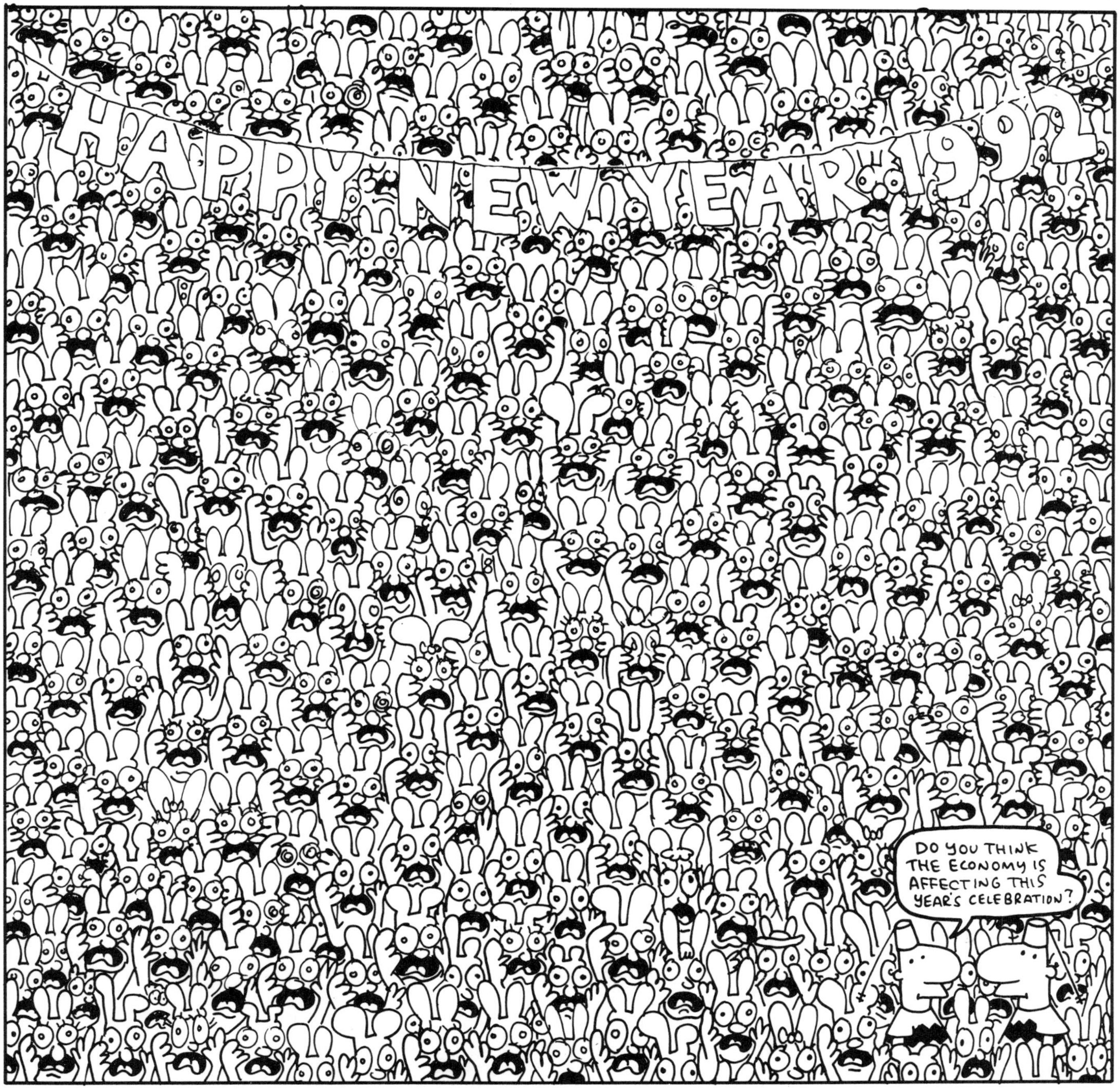

HAPPY NEW YEAR 1992
DO YOU THINK THE ECONOMY IS AFFECTING THIS YEAR'S CELEBRATION?

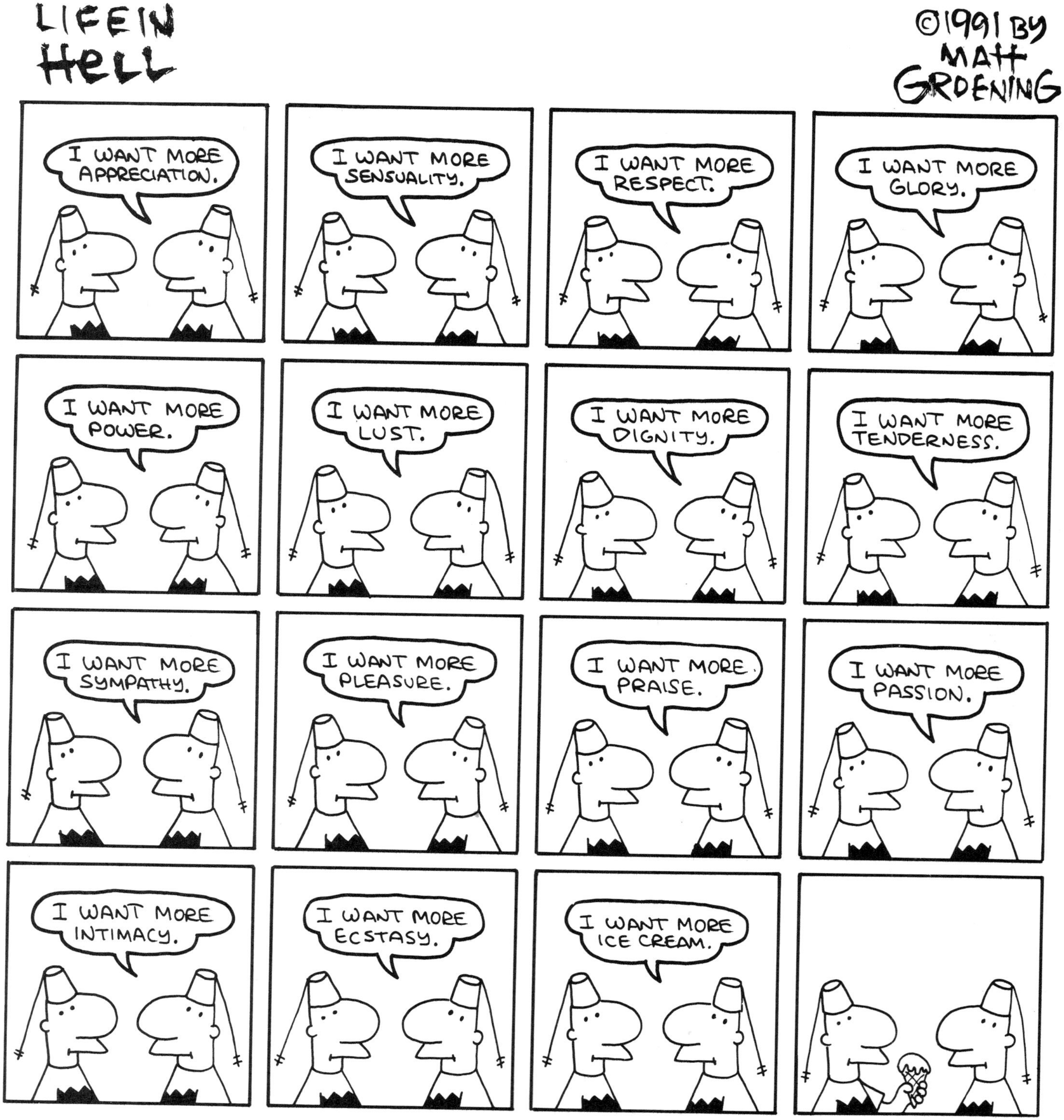
LIFE IN HELL
©1991 BY MATT GROENING
I WANT MORE APPRECIATION.
I WANT MORE SENSUALITY.
I WANT MORE RESPECT.
I WANT MORE GLORY.
I WANT MORE POWER.
I WANT MORE LUST.
I WANT MORE DIGNITY.
I WANT MORE TENDERNESS.
I WANT MORE SYMPATHY.
I WANT MORE PLEASURE.
I WANT MORE PRAISE.
I WANT MORE PASSION.
I WANT MORE INTIMACY.
I WANT MORE ECSTASY.
I WANT MORE ICE CREAM.

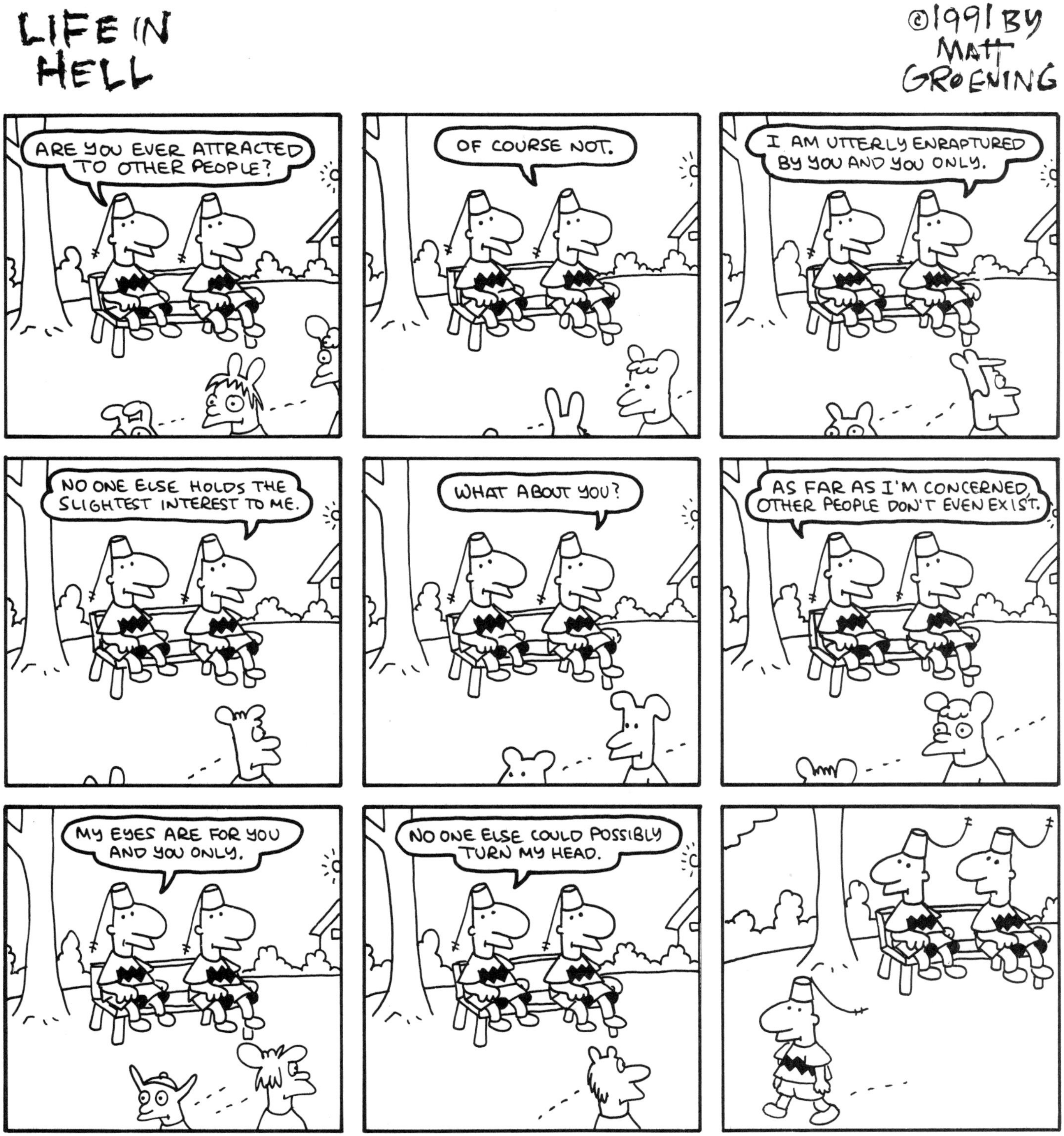
LIFE IN HELL
©1991 BY MATT GROENING
ARE YOU EVER ATTRACTED TO OTHER PEOPLE?
OF COURSE NOT.
I AM UTTERLY ENRAPTURED BY YOU AND YOU ONLY.
NO ONE ELSE HOLDS THE SLIGHTEST INTEREST TO ME.
WHAT ABOUT YOU?
AS FAR AS I'M CONCERNED, OTHER PEOPLE DON'T EVEN EXIST.
MY EYES ARE FOR YOU AND YOU ONLY.
NO ONE ELSE COULD POSSIBLY TURN MY HEAD.

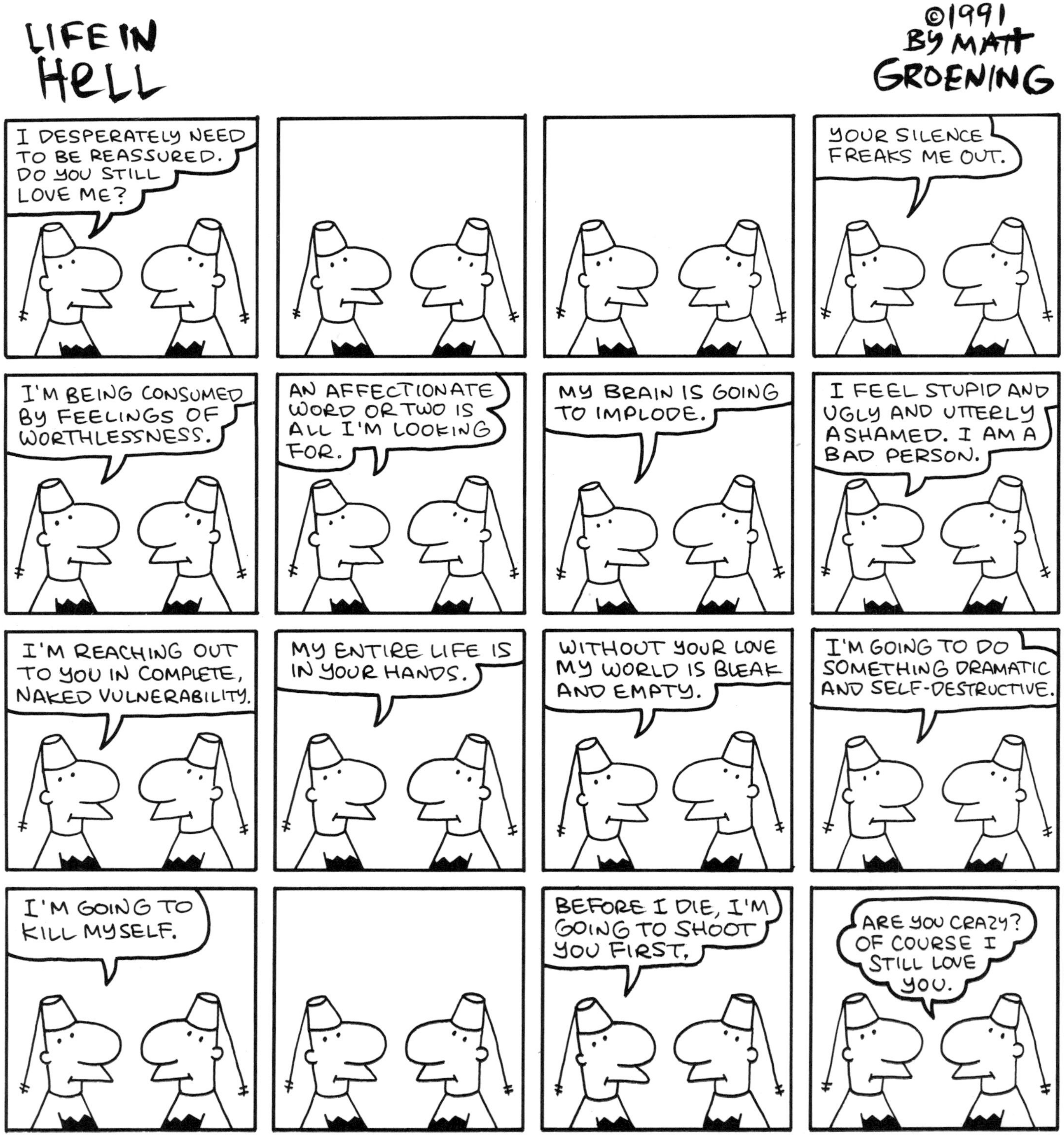
LIFE IN HELL
©1991 BY MATT GROENING
I DESPERATELY NEED TO BE REASSURED. DO YOU STILL LOVE ME?
YOUR SILENCE FREAKS ME OUT.
I'M BEING CONSUMED BY FEELINGS OF WORTHLESSNESS.
AN AFFECTIONATE WORD OR TWO IS ALL I'M LOOKING FOR.
MY BRAIN IS GOING TO IMPLODE.
I FEEL STUPID AND UGLY AND UTTERLY ASHAMED. I AM A BAD PERSON.
I'M REACHING OUT TO YOU IN COMPLETE, NAKED VULNERABILITY.
MY ENTIRE LIFE IS IN YOUR HANDS.
WITHOUT YOUR LOVE MY WORLD IS BLEAK AND EMPTY.
I'M GOING TO DO SOMETHING DRAMATIC AND SELF-DESTRUCTIVE.
I'M GOING TO KILL MYSELF.
BEFORE I DIE, I'M GOING TO SHOOT YOU FIRST.
ARE YOU CRAZY? OF COURSE I STILL LOVE YOU.

LIFE IN HELL

©1991 BY MATT GROENING

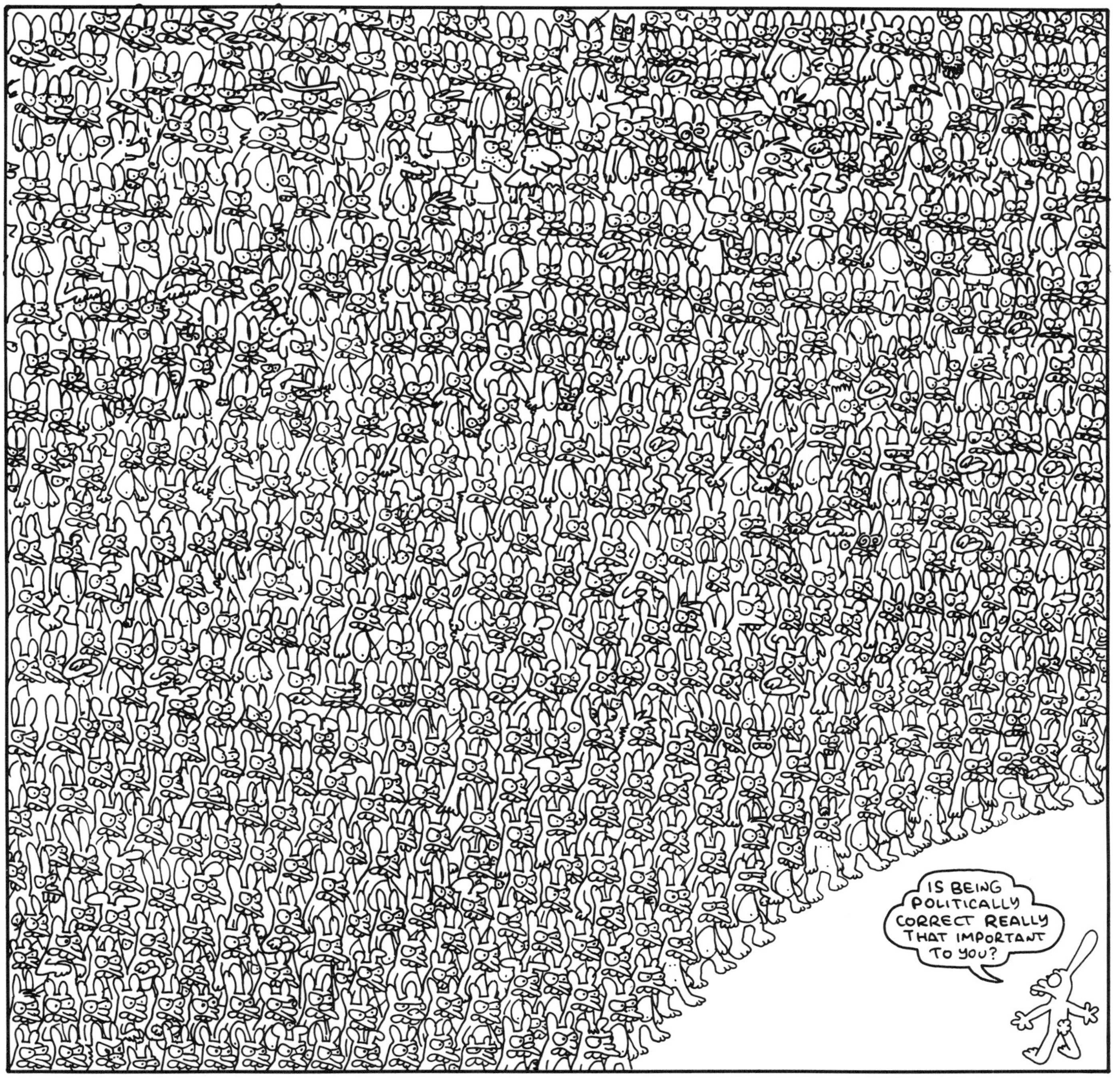
IS BEING POLITICALLY CORRECT REALLY THAT IMPORTANT TO YOU?

LIFE IN HELL

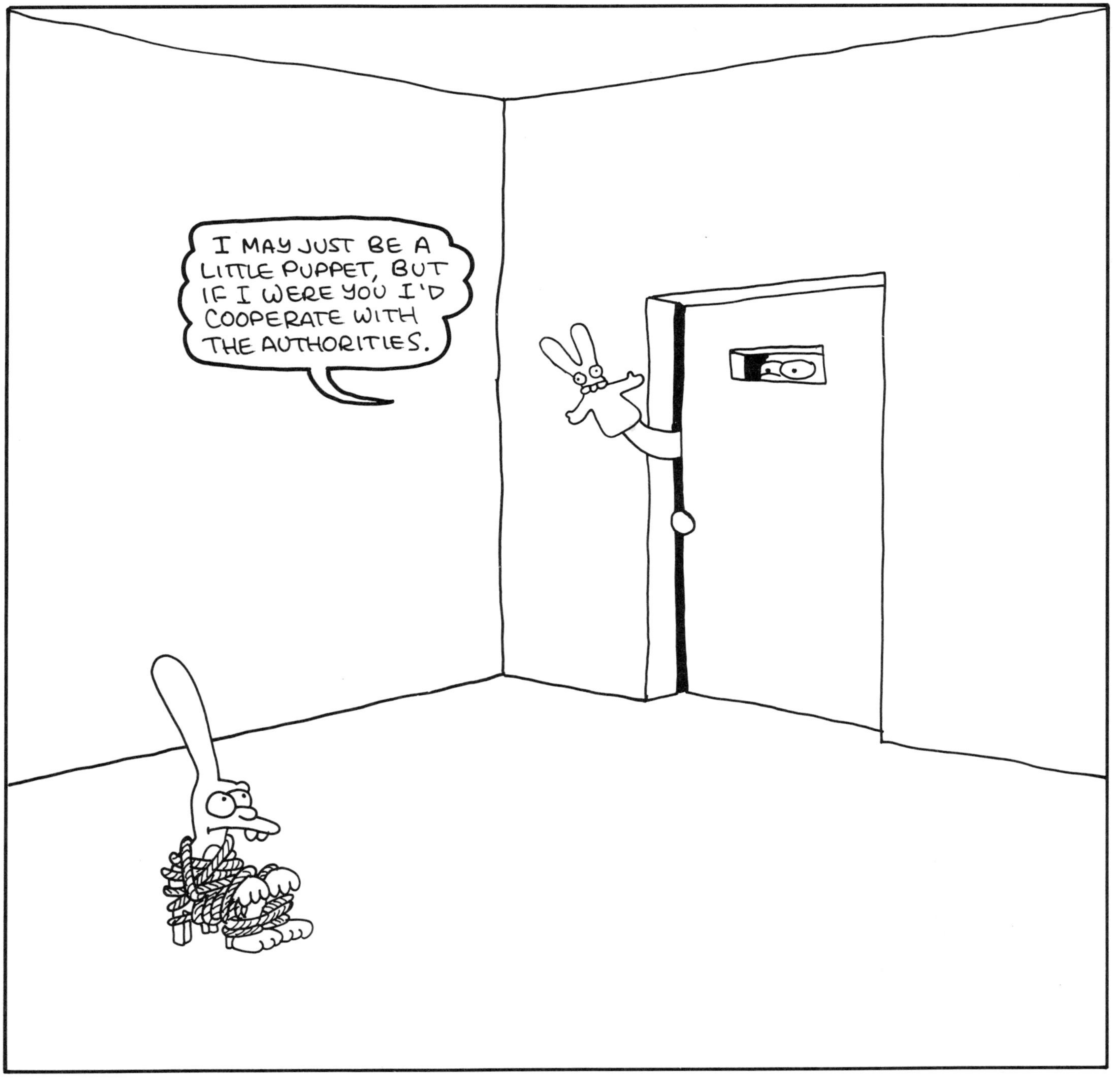
I MAY JUST BE A LITTLE PUPPET, BUT IF I WERE YOU I'D COOPERATE WITH THE AUTHORITIES.

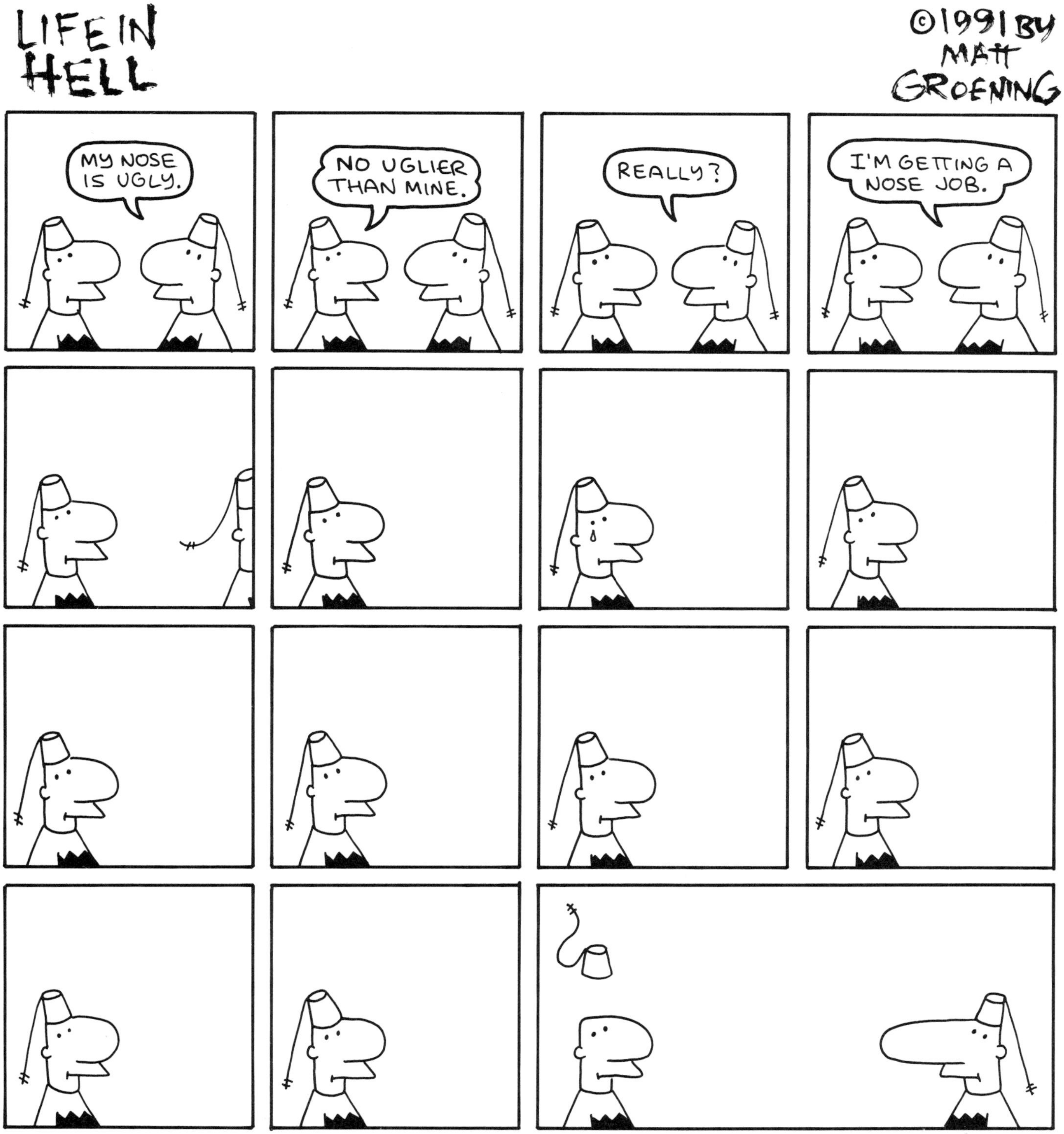
LIFE IN HELL
©1991 BY MATT GROENING
MY NOSE IS UGLY.
NO UGLIER THAN MINE.
REALLY?
I'M GETTING A NOSE JOB.

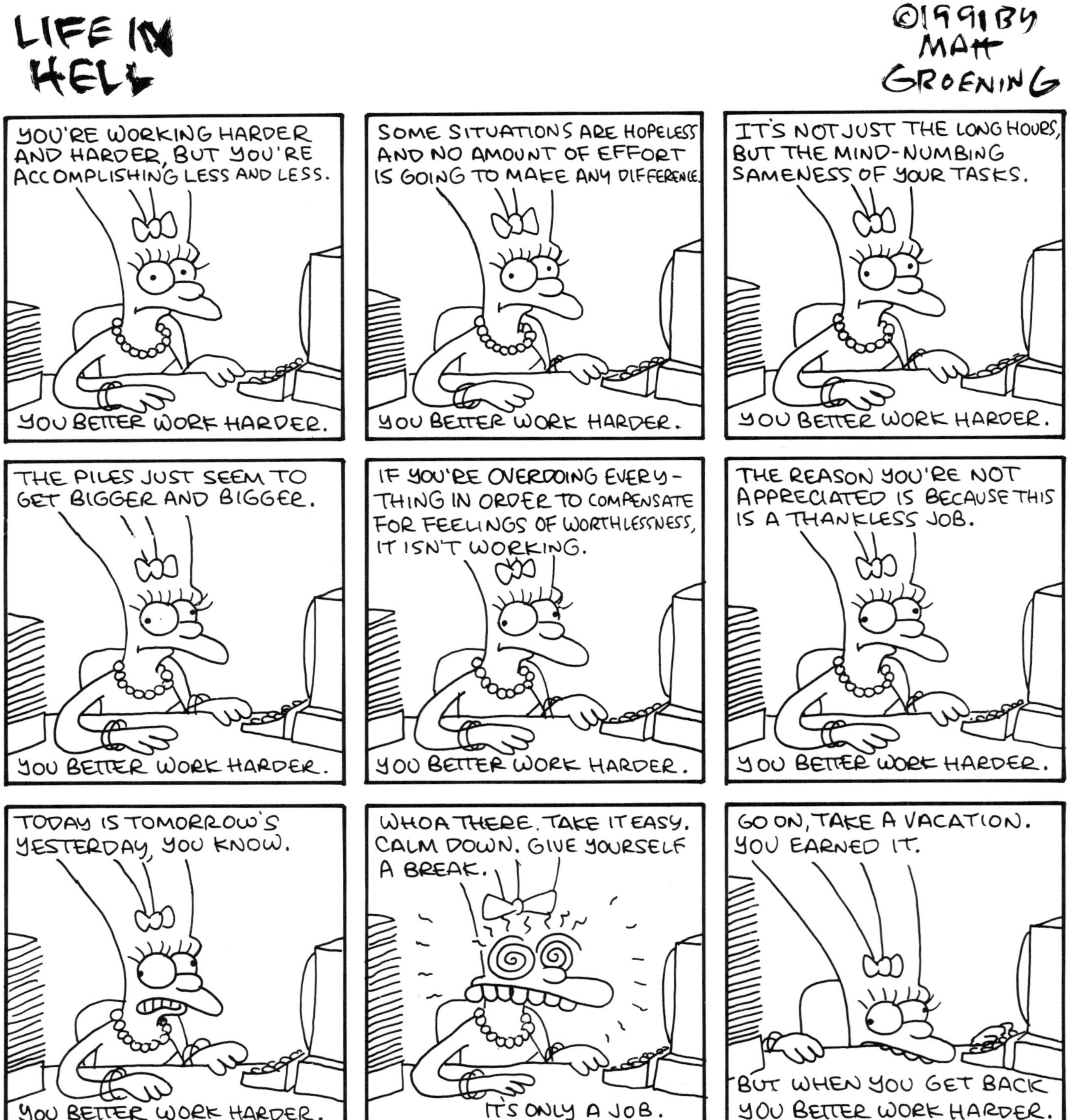
LIFE IN HELL
©1991 BY MATT GROENING
YOU'RE WORKING HARDER AND HARDER, BUT YOU'RE ACCOMPLISHING LESS AND LESS.
YOU BETTER WORK HARDER.
SOME SITUATIONS ARE HOPELESS AND NO AMOUNT OF EFFORT IS GOING TO MAKE ANY DIFFERENCE.
YOU BETTER WORK HARDER.
IT'S NOT JUST THE LONG HOURS, BUT THE MIND-NUMBING SAMENESS OF YOUR TASKS.
YOU BETTER WORK HARDER.
THE PILES JUST SEEM TO GET BIGGER AND BIGGER.
YOU BETTER WORK HARDER.
IF YOU'RE OVERDOING EVERY-THING IN ORDER TO COMPENSATE FOR FEELINGS OF WORTHLESSNESS, IT ISN'T WORKING.
YOU BETTER WORK HARDER.
THE REASON YOU'RE NOT APPRECIATED IS BECAUSE THIS IS A THANKLESS JOB.
YOU BETTER WORK HARDER.
TODAY IS TOMORROW'S YESTERDAY, YOU KNOW.
YOU BETTER WORK HARDER.
WHOA THERE. TAKE IT EASY. CALM DOWN. GIVE YOURSELF A BREAK.
IT'S ONLY A JOB.
GO ON, TAKE A VACATION. YOU EARNED IT.
BUT WHEN YOU GET BACK YOU BETTER WORK HARDER.

LIFE IN HELL

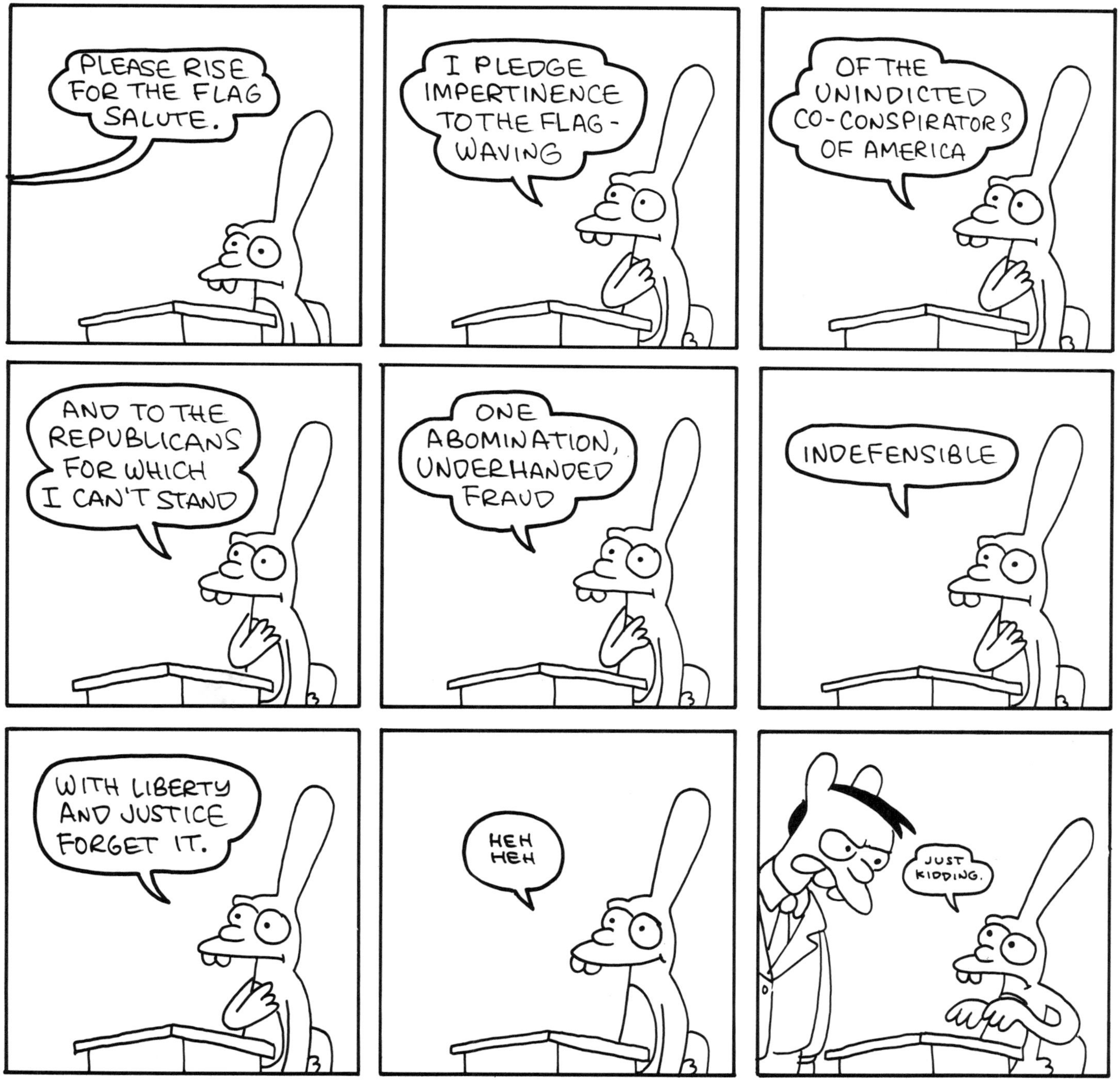
PLEASE RISE FOR THE FLAG SALUTE.
I PLEDGE IMPERTINENCE TO THE FLAG-WAVING
OF THE UNINDICTED CO-CONSPIRATORS OF AMERICA
AND TO THE REPUBLICANS FOR WHICH I CAN'T STAND
ONE ABOMINATION, UNDERHANDED FRAUD
INDEFENSIBLE
WITH LIBERTY AND JUSTICE FORGET IT.
HEH HEH
JUST KIDDING.

LIFE IN HELL

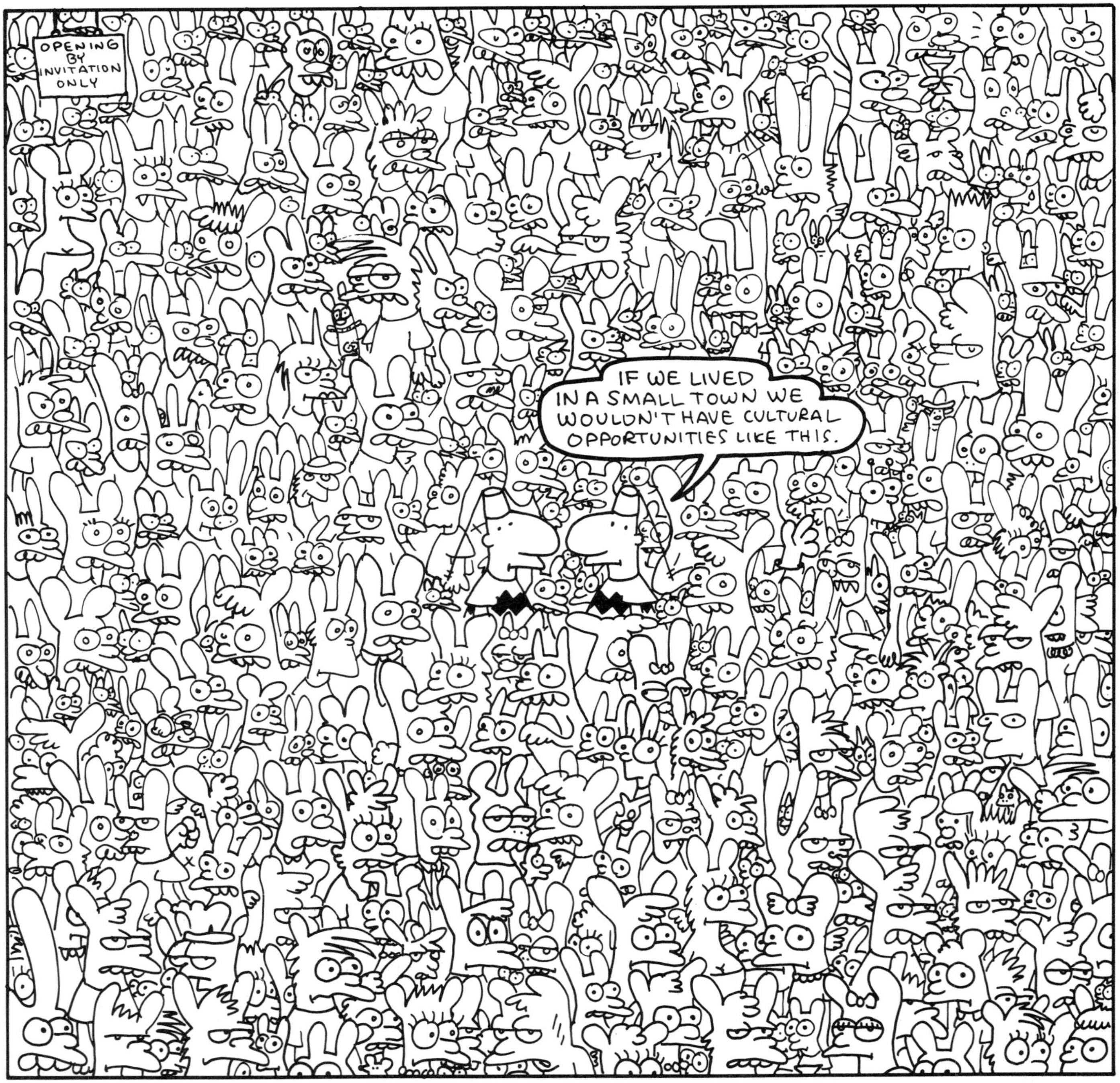
OPENING BY INVITATION ONLY
IF WE LIVED IN A SMALL TOWN WE WOULDN'T HAVE CULTURAL OPPORTUNITIES LIKE THIS.

LIFE IN HELL

©1991 BY MATT GROENING

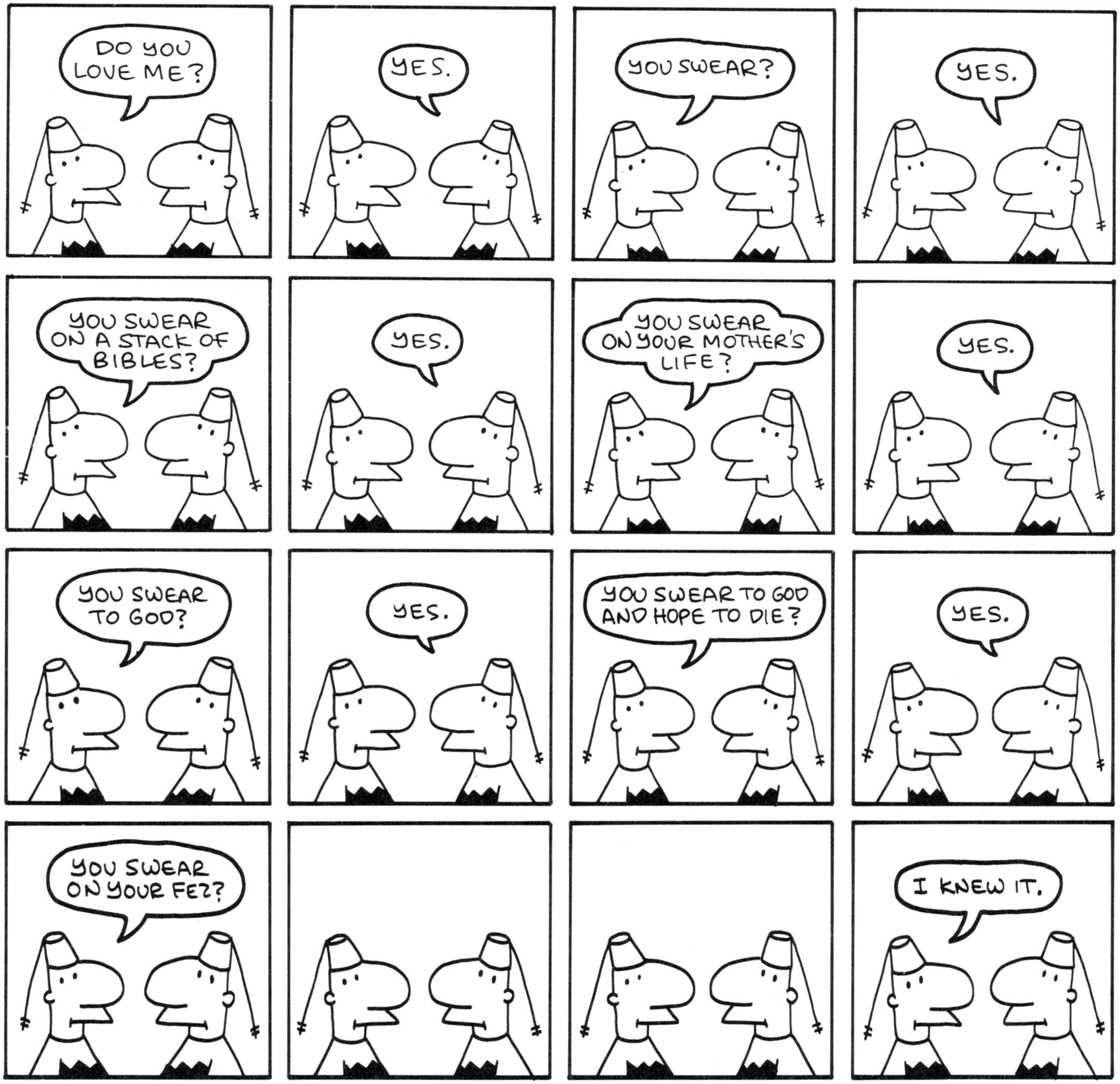
DO YOU LOVE ME?
YES.
YOU SWEAR?
YES.
YOU SWEAR ON A STACK OF BIBLES?
YES.
YOU SWEAR ON YOUR MOTHER'S LIFE?
YES.
YOU SWEAR TO GOD?
YES.
YOU SWEAR TO GOD AND HOPE TO DIE?
YES.
YOU SWEAR ON YOUR FEZ?
I KNEW IT.

LIFE IN HELL

THANKS TO DEBORAH CAPLAN, SARAH LA SAULLE, MARY TRAINOR, CINDY VANCE, STEVE VANCE, AND MILI SMYTHE

FORBIDDEN WORDS OF 1992

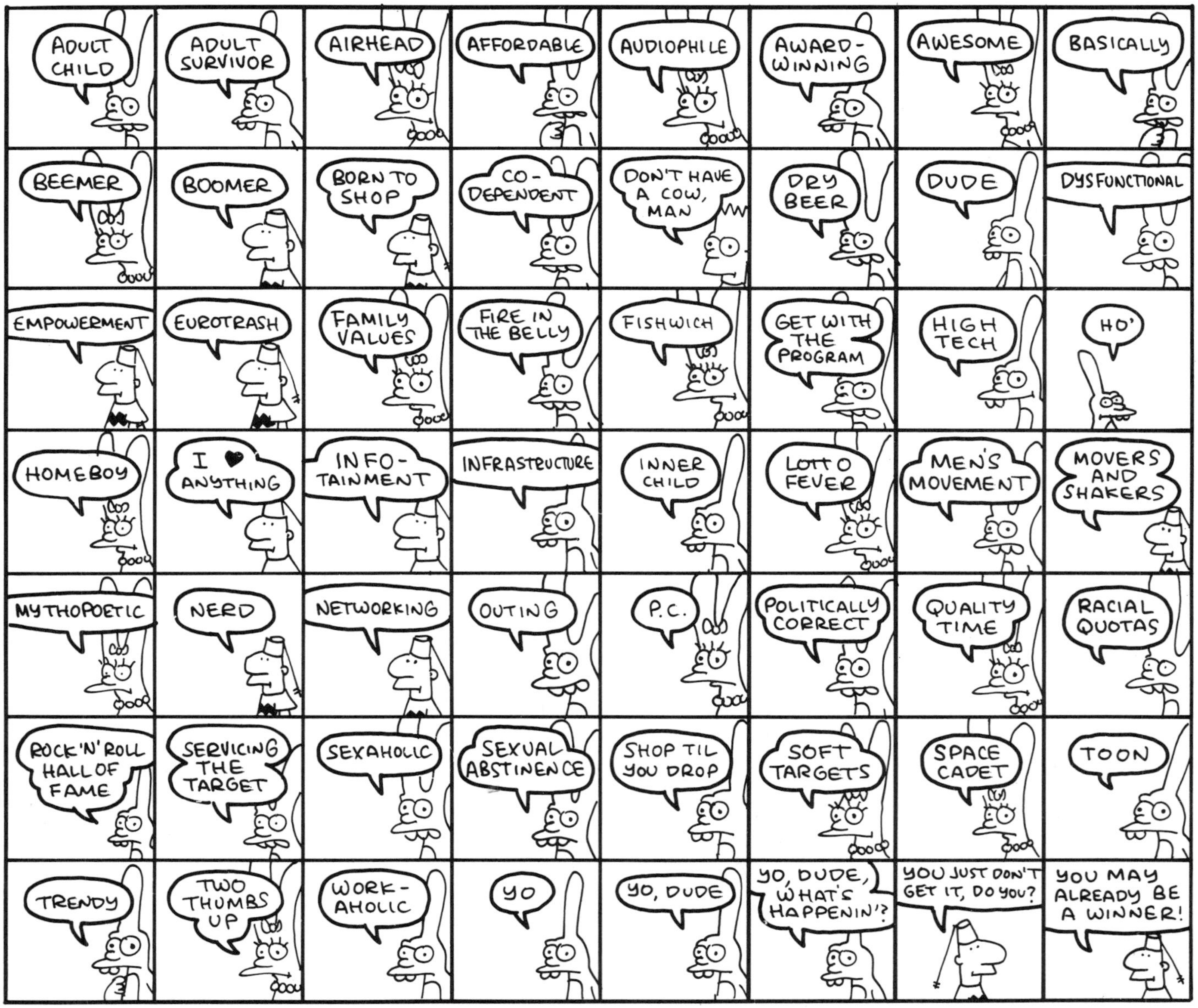
ADULT CHILD
ADULT SURVIVOR
AIRHEAD
AFFORDABLE
AUDIOPHILE
AWARD-WINNING
AWESOME
BASICALLY
BEEMER
BOOMER
BORN TO SHOP
CO-DEPENDENT
DON'T HAVE A COW, MAN
DRY BEER
DUDE
DYSFUNCTIONAL
EMPOWERMENT
EUROTRASH
FAMILY VALUES
FIRE IN THE BELLY
FISHWICH
GET WITH THE PROGRAM
HIGH TECH
HO'
HOMEBOY
I ♥ ANYTHING
INFO-TAINMENT
INFRASTRUCTURE
INNER CHILD
LOTTO FEVER
MEN'S MOVEMENT
MOVERS AND SHAKERS
MYTHOPOETIC
NERD
NETWORKING
OUTING
P.C.
POLITICALLY CORRECT
QUALITY TIME
RACIAL QUOTAS
ROCK 'N' ROLL HALL OF FAME
SERVICING THE TARGET
SEXAHOLIC
SEXUAL ABSTINENCE
SHOP TIL YOU DROP
SOFT TARGETS
SPACE CADET
TOON
TRENDY
TWO THUMBS UP
WORK-AHOLIC
YO
YO, DUDE
YO, DUDE, WHAT'S HAPPENIN'?
YOU JUST DON'T GET IT, DO YOU?
YOU MAY ALREADY BE A WINNER!

LIFE IN HELL

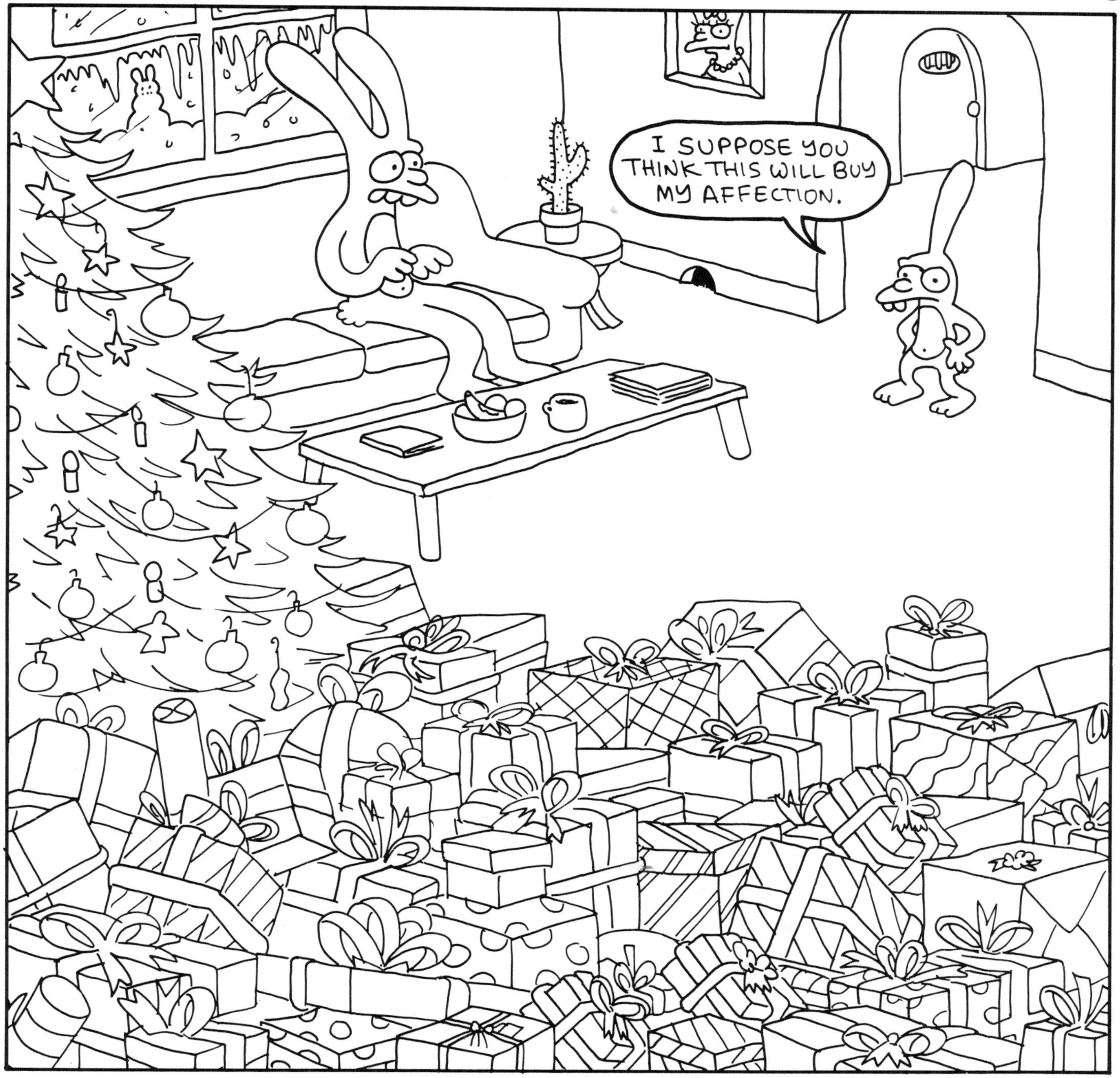
I SUPPOSE YOU THINK THIS WILL BUY MY AFFECTION.

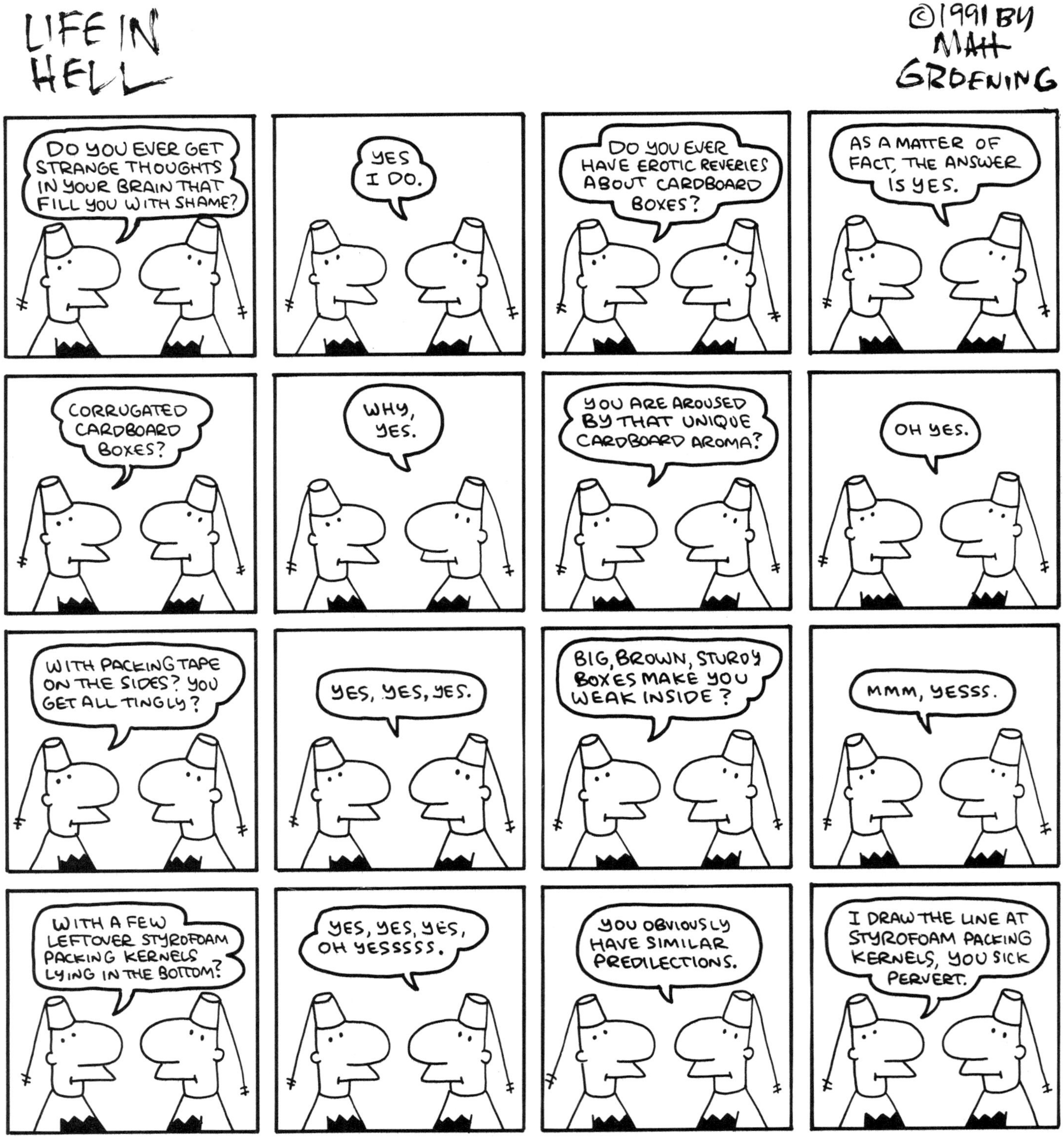
LIFE IN HELL
©1991 BY MATT GROENING
DO YOU EVER GET STRANGE THOUGHTS IN YOUR BRAIN THAT FILL YOU WITH SHAME?
YES I DO.
DO YOU EVER HAVE EROTIC REVERIES ABOUT CARDBOARD BOXES?
AS A MATTER OF FACT, THE ANSWER IS YES.
CORRUGATED CARDBOARD BOXES?
WHY, YES.
YOU ARE AROUSED BY THAT UNIQUE CARDBOARD AROMA?
OH YES.
WITH PACKING TAPE ON THE SIDES? YOU GET ALL TINGLY?
YES, YES, YES.
BIG, BROWN, STURDY BOXES MAKE YOU WEAK INSIDE?
MMM, YESSS.
WITH A FEW LEFTOVER STYROFOAM PACKING KERNELS LYING IN THE BOTTOM?
YES, YES, YES, OH YESSSSS.
YOU OBVIOUSLY HAVE SIMILAR PREDILECTIONS.
I DRAW THE LINE AT STYROFOAM PACKING KERNELS, YOU SICK PERVERT.

LIFE IN HELL

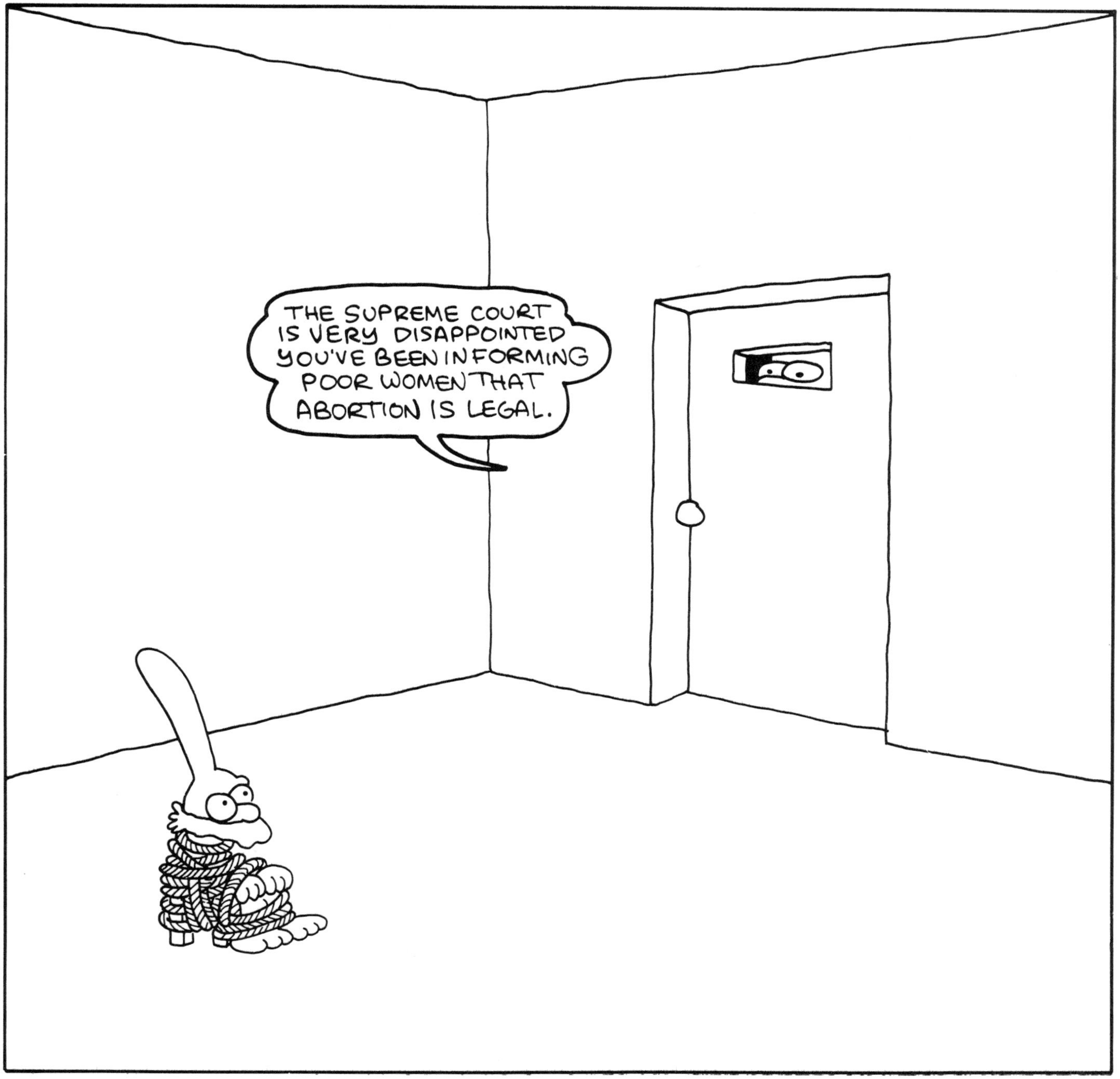
THE SUPREME COURT IS VERY DISAPPOINTED YOU'VE BEEN INFORMING POOR WOMEN THAT ABORTION IS LEGAL.

LIFE IN HELL

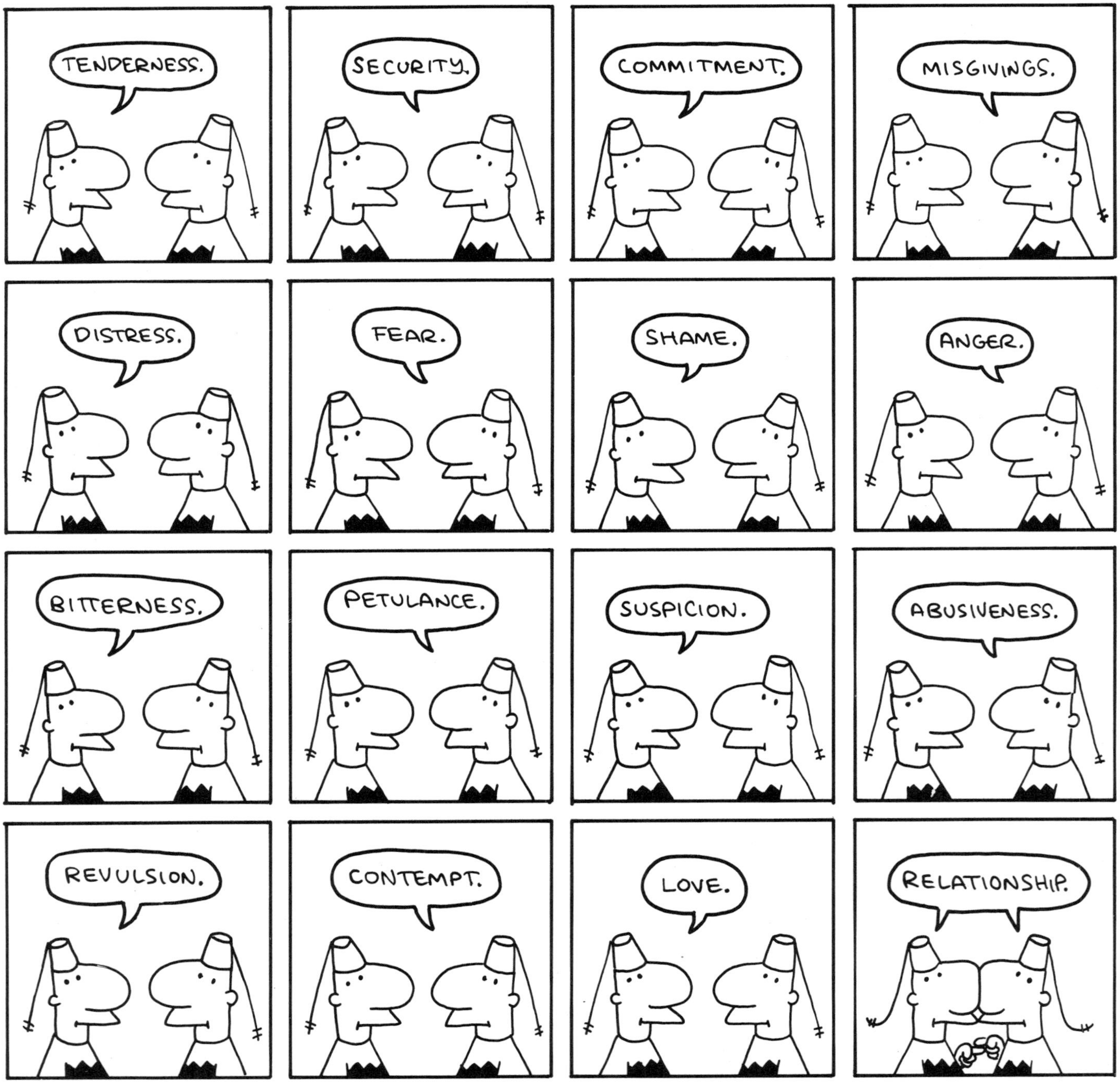
TENDERNESS.
SECURITY.
COMMITMENT.
MISGIVINGS.
DISTRESS.
FEAR.
SHAME.
ANGER.
BITTERNESS.
PETULANCE.
SUSPICION.
ABUSIVENESS.
REVULSION.
CONTEMPT.
LOVE.
RELATIONSHIP.

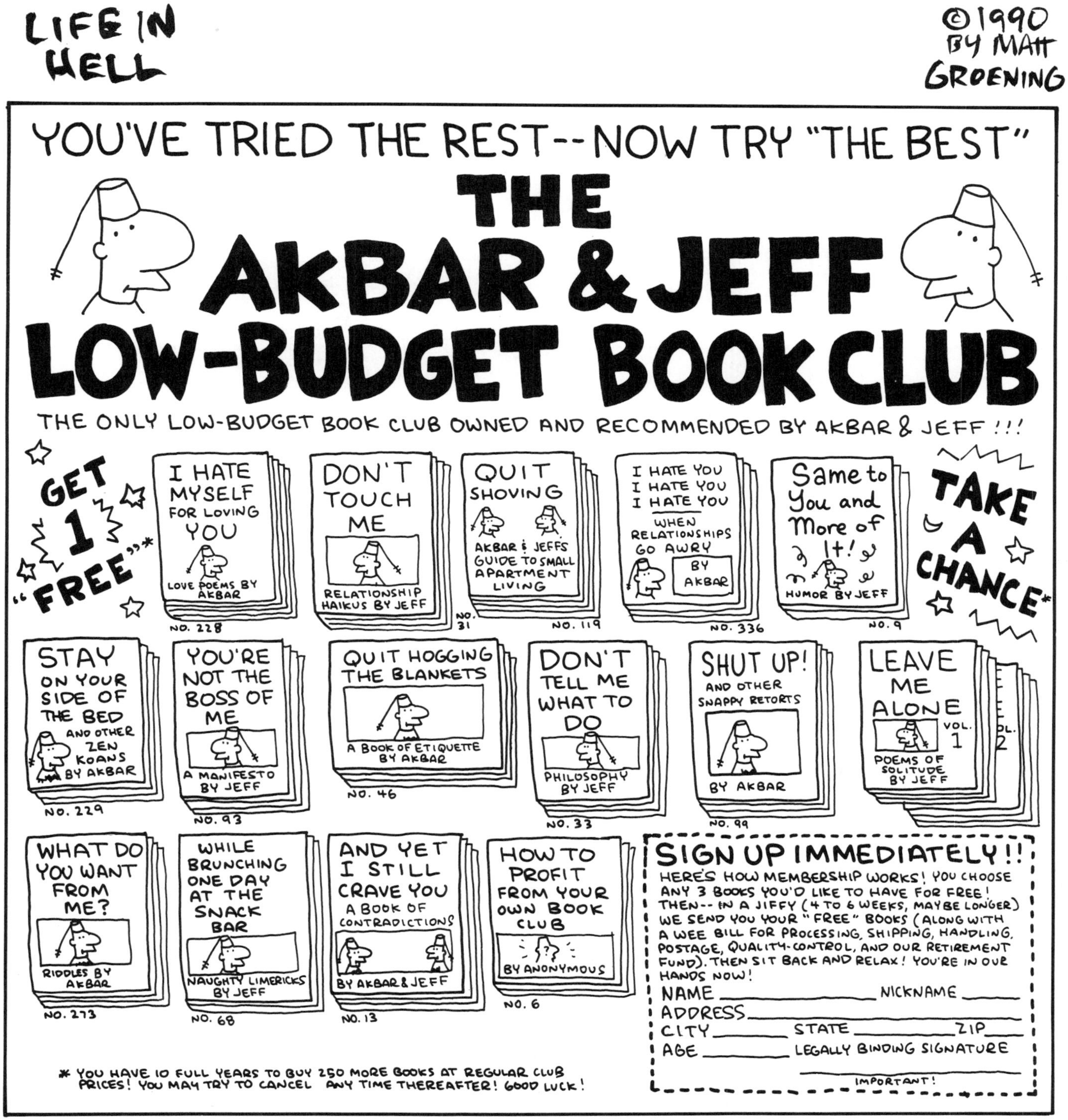
LIFE IN HELL
©1990 BY MATT GROENING
YOU'VE TRIED THE REST--NOW TRY "THE BEST"
THE AKBAR & JEFF LOW-BUDGET BOOK CLUB
THE ONLY LOW-BUDGET BOOK CLUB OWNED AND RECOMMENDED BY AKBAR & JEFF!!!
GET 1 "FREE"*
TAKE A CHANCE*
I HATE MYSELF FOR LOVING YOU
LOVE POEMS BY AKBAR
NO. 228
DON'T TOUCH ME
RELATIONSHIP HAIKUS BY JEFF
NO. 31
QUIT SHOVING
AKBAR & JEFFS GUIDE TO SMALL APARTMENT LIVING
NO. 119
I HATE YOU I HATE YOU I HATE YOU
WHEN RELATIONSHIPS GO AWRY
BY AKBAR
NO. 336
Same to You and More of It!
HUMOR BY JEFF
NO. 9
STAY ON YOUR SIDE OF THE BED
AND OTHER ZEN KOANS BY AKBAR
NO. 229
YOU'RE NOT THE BOSS OF ME
A MANIFESTO BY JEFF
NO. 93
QUIT HOGGING THE BLANKETS
A BOOK OF ETIQUETTE BY AKBAR
NO. 46
DON'T TELL ME WHAT TO DO
PHILOSOPHY BY JEFF
NO. 33
SHUT UP!
AND OTHER SNAPPY RETORTS
BY AKBAR
NO. 99
LEAVE ME ALONE
VOL. 1
POEMS OF SOLITUDE BY JEFF
WHAT DO YOU WANT FROM ME?
RIDDLES BY AKBAR
NO. 273
WHILE BRUNCHING ONE DAY AT THE SNACK BAR
NAUGHTY LIMERICKS BY JEFF
NO. 68
AND YET I STILL CRAVE YOU
A BOOK OF CONTRADICTIONS
BY AKBAR & JEFF
NO. 13
HOW TO PROFIT FROM YOUR OWN BOOK CLUB
BY ANONYMOUS
NO. 6
SIGN UP IMMEDIATELY!!
HERE'S HOW MEMBERSHIP WORKS! YOU CHOOSE ANY 3 BOOKS YOU'D LIKE TO HAVE FOR FREE! THEN-- IN A JIFFY (4 TO 6 WEEKS, MAYBE LONGER) WE SEND YOU YOUR "FREE" BOOKS (ALONG WITH A WEE BILL FOR PROCESSING, SHIPPING, HANDLING, POSTAGE, QUALITY-CONTROL, AND OUR RETIREMENT FUND). THEN SIT BACK AND RELAX! YOU'RE IN OUR HANDS NOW!
NAME ________ NICKNAME ____
ADDRESS ________
CITY ____ STATE ____ ZIP ____
AGE ____ LEGALLY BINDING SIGNATURE
IMPORTANT!
* YOU HAVE 10 FULL YEARS TO BUY 250 MORE BOOKS AT REGULAR CLUB PRICES! YOU MAY TRY TO CANCEL ANY TIME THEREAFTER! GOOD LUCK!

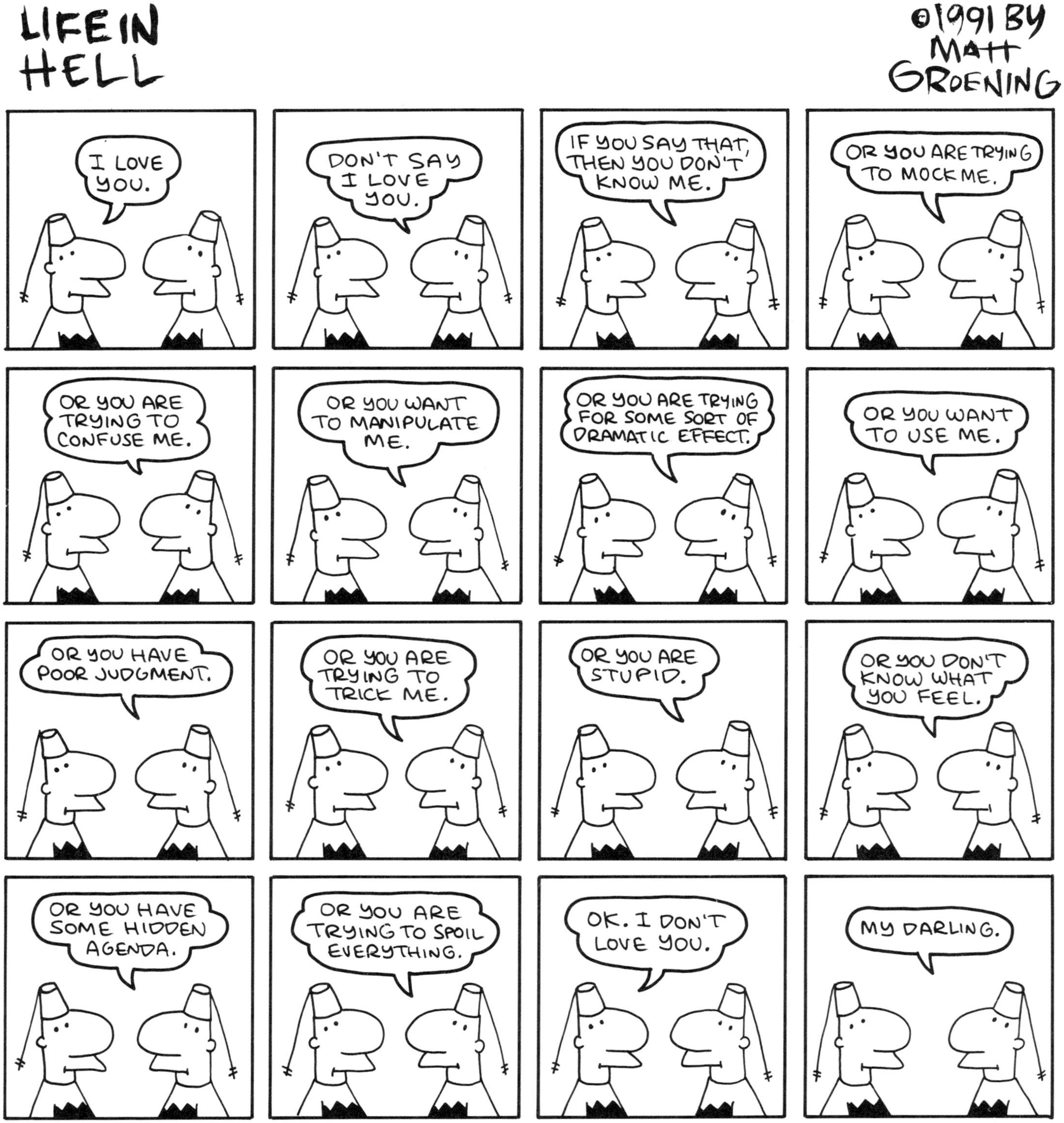
LIFE IN HELL
©1991 BY MATT GROENING
I LOVE YOU.
DON'T SAY I LOVE YOU.
IF YOU SAY THAT, THEN YOU DON'T KNOW ME.
OR YOU ARE TRYING TO MOCK ME.
OR YOU ARE TRYING TO CONFUSE ME.
OR YOU WANT TO MANIPULATE ME.
OR YOU ARE TRYING FOR SOME SORT OF DRAMATIC EFFECT.
OR YOU WANT TO USE ME.
OR YOU HAVE POOR JUDGMENT.
OR YOU ARE TRYING TO TRICK ME.
OR YOU ARE STUPID.
OR YOU DON'T KNOW WHAT YOU FEEL.
OR YOU HAVE SOME HIDDEN AGENDA.
OR YOU ARE TRYING TO SPOIL EVERYTHING.
OK. I DON'T LOVE YOU.
MY DARLING.

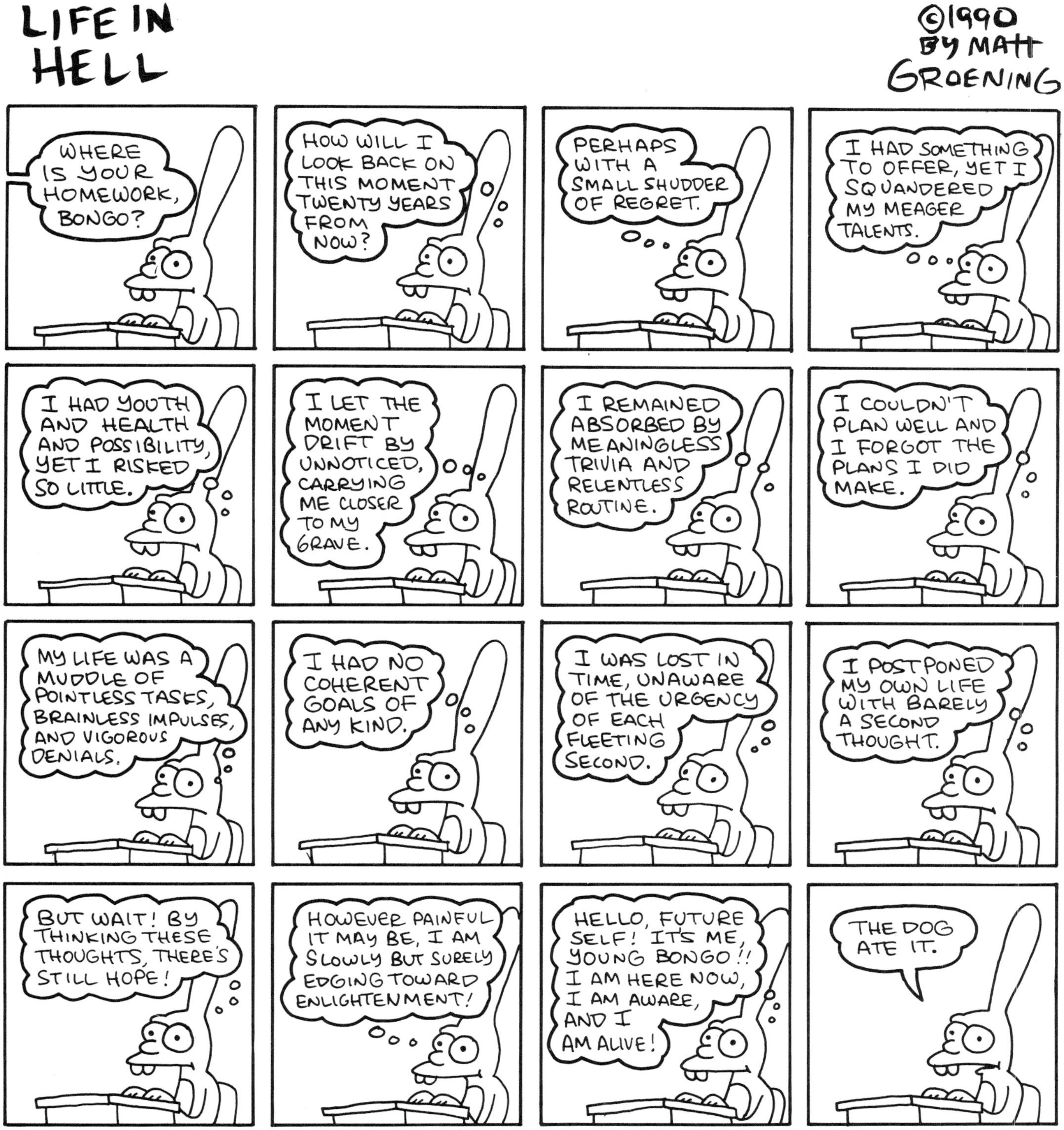
LIFE IN HELL
©1990 BY MATT GROENING
WHERE IS YOUR HOMEWORK, BONGO?
HOW WILL I LOOK BACK ON THIS MOMENT TWENTY YEARS FROM NOW?
PERHAPS WITH A SMALL SHUDDER OF REGRET.
I HAD SOMETHING TO OFFER, YET I SQUANDERED MY MEAGER TALENTS.
I HAD YOUTH AND HEALTH AND POSSIBILITY, YET I RISKED SO LITTLE.
I LET THE MOMENT DRIFT BY UNNOTICED, CARRYING ME CLOSER TO MY GRAVE.
I REMAINED ABSORBED BY MEANINGLESS TRIVIA AND RELENTLESS ROUTINE.
I COULDN'T PLAN WELL AND I FORGOT THE PLANS I DID MAKE.
MY LIFE WAS A MUDDLE OF POINTLESS TASKS, BRAINLESS IMPULSES, AND VIGOROUS DENIALS.
I HAD NO COHERENT GOALS OF ANY KIND.
I WAS LOST IN TIME, UNAWARE OF THE URGENCY OF EACH FLEETING SECOND.
I POSTPONED MY OWN LIFE WITH BARELY A SECOND THOUGHT.
BUT WAIT! BY THINKING THESE THOUGHTS, THERE'S STILL HOPE!
HOWEVER PAINFUL IT MAY BE, I AM SLOWLY BUT SURELY EDGING TOWARD ENLIGHTENMENT!
HELLO, FUTURE SELF! IT'S ME, YOUNG BONGO!! I AM HERE NOW, I AM AWARE, AND I AM ALIVE!
THE DOG ATE IT.

LIFE IN HELL

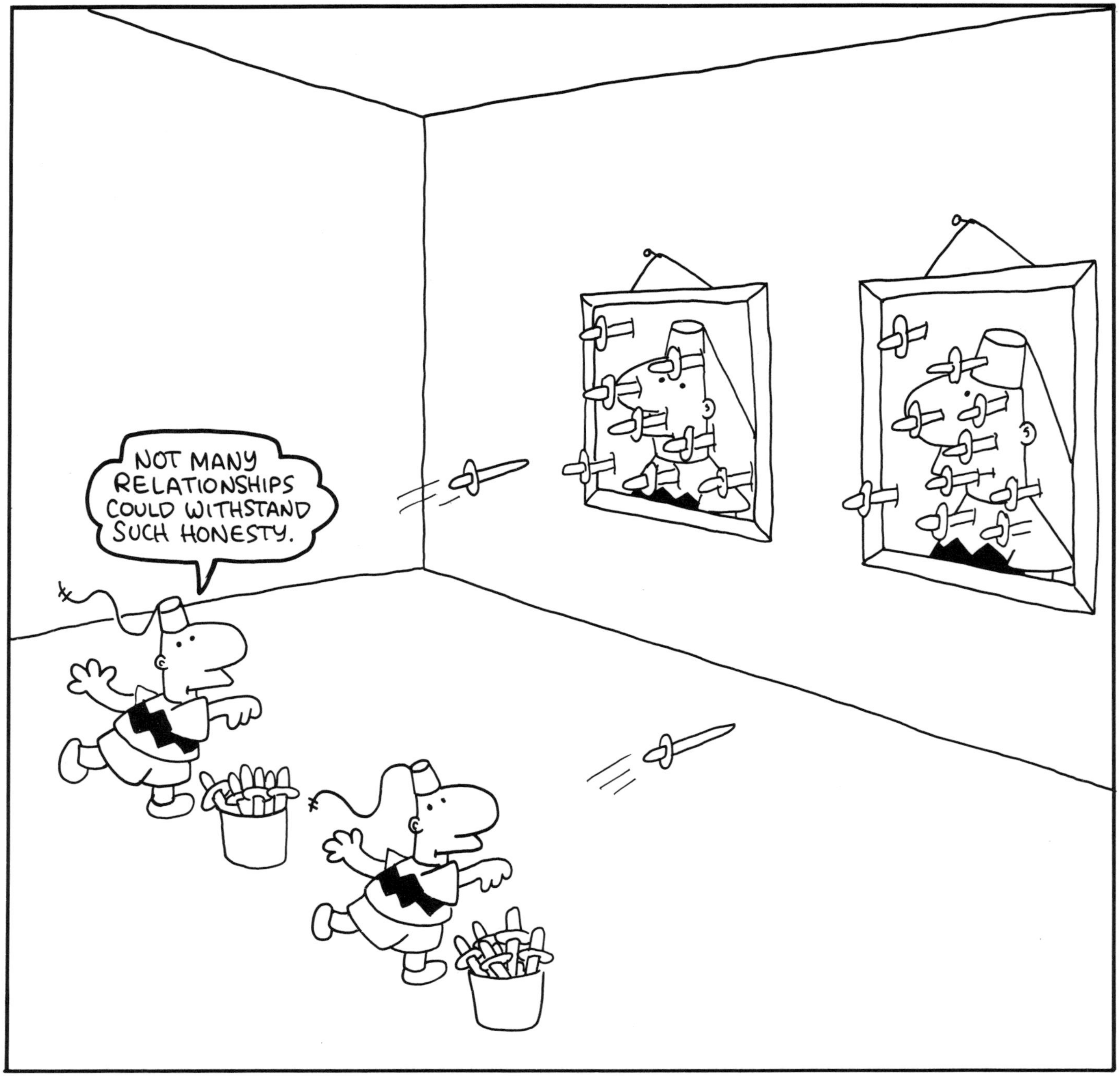
NOT MANY RELATIONSHIPS COULD WITHSTAND SUCH HONESTY.

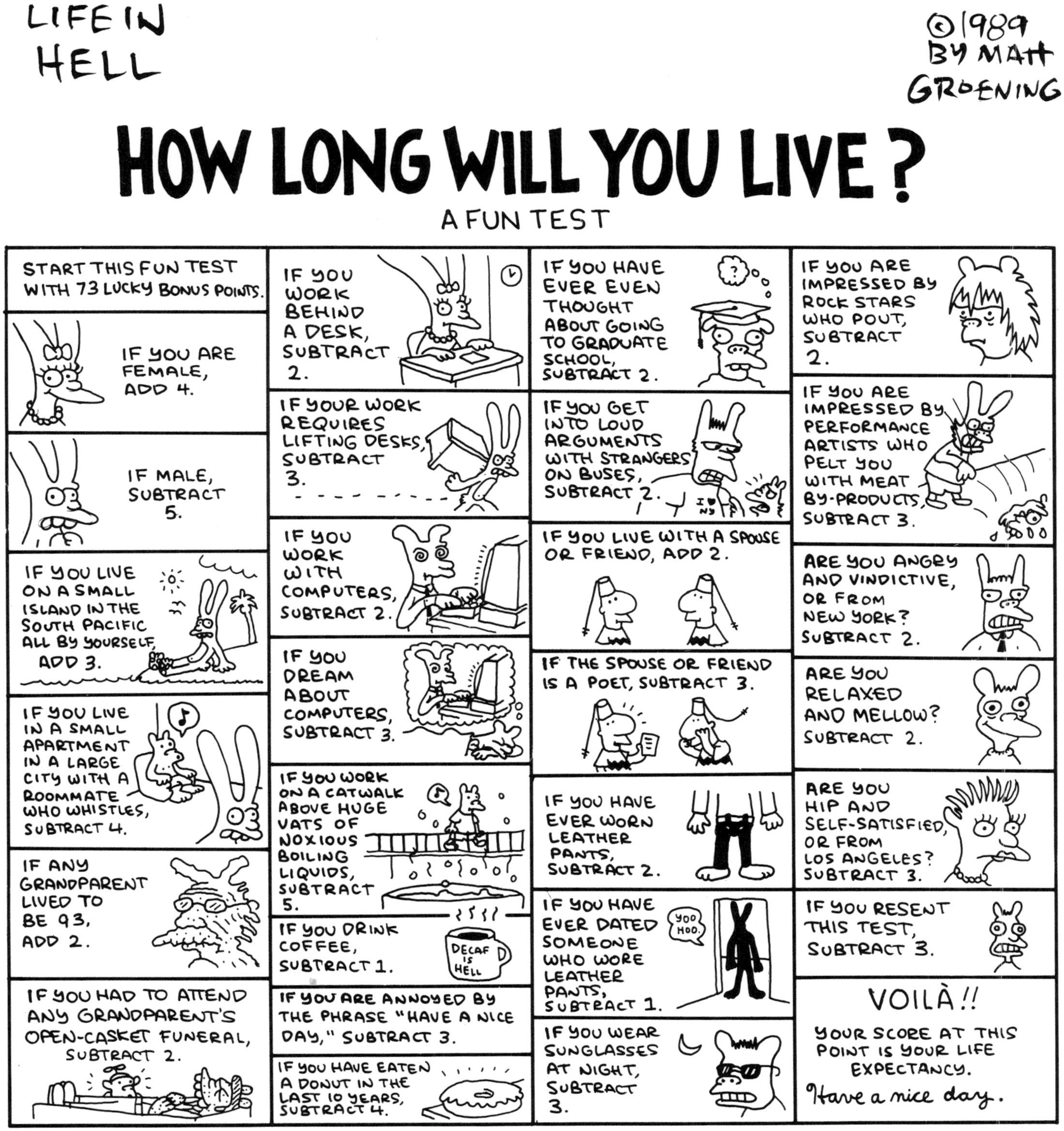
LIFE IN HELL
©1989 BY MATT GROENING
HOW LONG WILL YOU LIVE?
A FUN TEST
START THIS FUN TEST WITH 73 LUCKY BONUS POINTS.
IF YOU ARE FEMALE, ADD 4.
IF MALE, SUBTRACT 5.
IF YOU LIVE ON A SMALL ISLAND IN THE SOUTH PACIFIC ALL BY YOURSELF, ADD 3.
IF YOU LIVE IN A SMALL APARTMENT IN A LARGE CITY WITH A ROOMMATE WHO WHISTLES, SUBTRACT 4.
IF ANY GRANDPARENT LIVED TO BE 93, ADD 2.
IF YOU HAD TO ATTEND ANY GRANDPARENT'S OPEN-CASKET FUNERAL, SUBTRACT 2.
IF YOU WORK BEHIND A DESK, SUBTRACT 2.
IF YOUR WORK REQUIRES LIFTING DESKS, SUBTRACT 3.
IF YOU WORK WITH COMPUTERS, SUBTRACT 2.
IF YOU DREAM ABOUT COMPUTERS, SUBTRACT 3.
IF YOU WORK ON A CATWALK ABOVE HUGE VATS OF NOXIOUS BOILING LIQUIDS, SUBTRACT 5.
IF YOU DRINK COFFEE, SUBTRACT 1.
DECAF IS HELL
IF YOU ARE ANNOYED BY THE PHRASE "HAVE A NICE DAY," SUBTRACT 3.
IF YOU HAVE EATEN A DONUT IN THE LAST 10 YEARS, SUBTRACT 4.
IF YOU HAVE EVER EVEN THOUGHT ABOUT GOING TO GRADUATE SCHOOL, SUBTRACT 2.
IF YOU GET INTO LOUD ARGUMENTS WITH STRANGERS ON BUSES, SUBTRACT 2.
I ♥ NY
IF YOU LIVE WITH A SPOUSE OR FRIEND, ADD 2.
IF THE SPOUSE OR FRIEND IS A POET, SUBTRACT 3.
IF YOU HAVE EVER WORN LEATHER PANTS, SUBTRACT 2.
IF YOU HAVE EVER DATED SOMEONE WHO WORE LEATHER PANTS, SUBTRACT 1.
YOO HOO.
IF YOU WEAR SUNGLASSES AT NIGHT, SUBTRACT 3.
IF YOU ARE IMPRESSED BY ROCK STARS WHO POUT, SUBTRACT 2.
IF YOU ARE IMPRESSED BY PERFORMANCE ARTISTS WHO PELT YOU WITH MEAT BY-PRODUCTS, SUBTRACT 3.
ARE YOU ANGRY AND VINDICTIVE, OR FROM NEW YORK? SUBTRACT 2.
ARE YOU RELAXED AND MELLOW? SUBTRACT 2.
ARE YOU HIP AND SELF-SATISFIED, OR FROM LOS ANGELES? SUBTRACT 3.
IF YOU RESENT THIS TEST, SUBTRACT 3.
VOILÀ!!
YOUR SCORE AT THIS POINT IS YOUR LIFE EXPECTANCY.
Have a nice day.

LIFE IN HELL

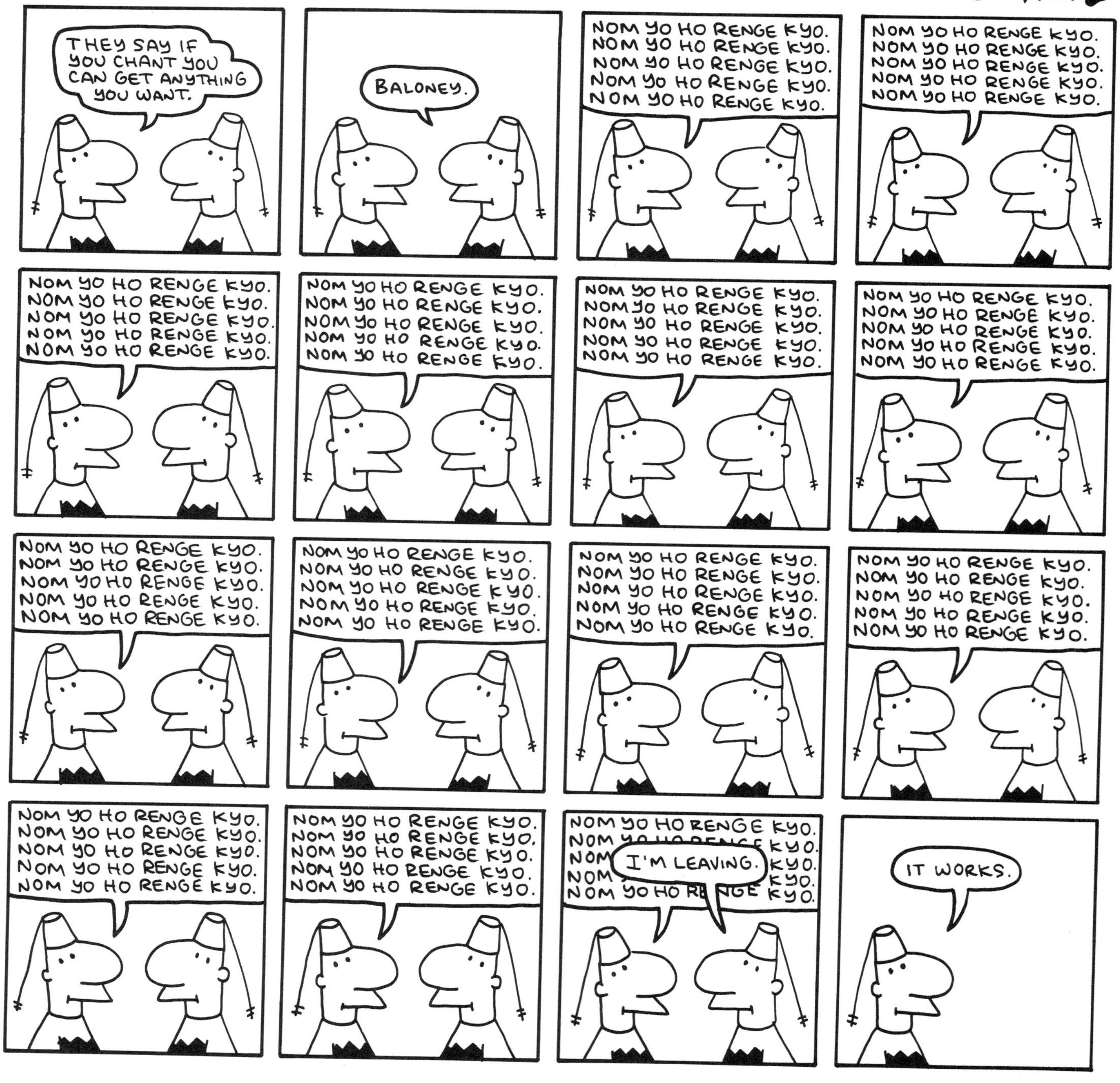
THEY SAY IF YOU CHANT YOU CAN GET ANYTHING YOU WANT.
BALONEY.
NOM YO HO RENGE KYO. NOM YO HO RENGE KYO. NOM YO HO RENGE KYO. NOM YO HO RENGE KYO. NOM YO HO RENGE KYO.
NOM YO HO RENGE KYO. NOM YO HO RENGE KYO. NOM YO HO RENGE KYO. NOM YO HO RENGE KYO. NOM YO HO RENGE KYO.
NOM YO HO RENGE KYO. NOM YO HO RENGE KYO. NOM YO HO RENGE KYO. NOM YO HO RENGE KYO. NOM YO HO RENGE KYO.
NOM YO HO RENGE KYO. NOM YO HO RENGE KYO. NOM YO HO RENGE KYO. NOM YO HO RENGE KYO. NOM YO HO RENGE KYO.
NOM YO HO RENGE KYO. NOM YO HO RENGE KYO. NOM YO HO RENGE KYO. NOM YO HO RENGE KYO. NOM YO HO RENGE KYO.
NOM YO HO RENGE KYO. NOM YO HO RENGE KYO. NOM YO HO RENGE KYO. NOM YO HO RENGE KYO. NOM YO HO RENGE KYO.
NOM YO HO RENGE KYO. NOM YO HO RENGE KYO. NOM YO HO RENGE KYO. NOM YO HO RENGE KYO. NOM YO HO RENGE KYO.
NOM YO HO RENGE KYO. NOM YO HO RENGE KYO. NOM YO HO RENGE KYO. NOM YO HO RENGE KYO. NOM YO HO RENGE KYO.
NOM YO HO RENGE KYO. NOM YO HO RENGE KYO. NOM YO HO RENGE KYO. NOM YO HO RENGE KYO. NOM YO HO RENGE KYO.
NOM YO HO RENGE KYO. NOM YO HO RENGE KYO. NOM YO HO RENGE KYO. NOM YO HO RENGE KYO. NOM YO HO RENGE KYO.
NOM YO HO RENGE KYO. NOM YO HO RENGE KYO. NOM YO HO RENGE KYO. NOM YO HO RENGE KYO. NOM YO HO RENGE KYO.
NOM YO HO RENGE KYO. NOM YO HO RENGE KYO. NOM YO HO RENGE KYO. NOM YO HO RENGE KYO. NOM YO HO RENGE KYO.
NOM YO HO RENGE KYO. NOM YO HO RENGE KYO. NOM YO HO RENGE KYO. NOM YO HO RENGE KYO. NOM YO HO RENGE KYO.
NOM YO HO RENGE KYO.
I'M LEAVING.
IT WORKS.

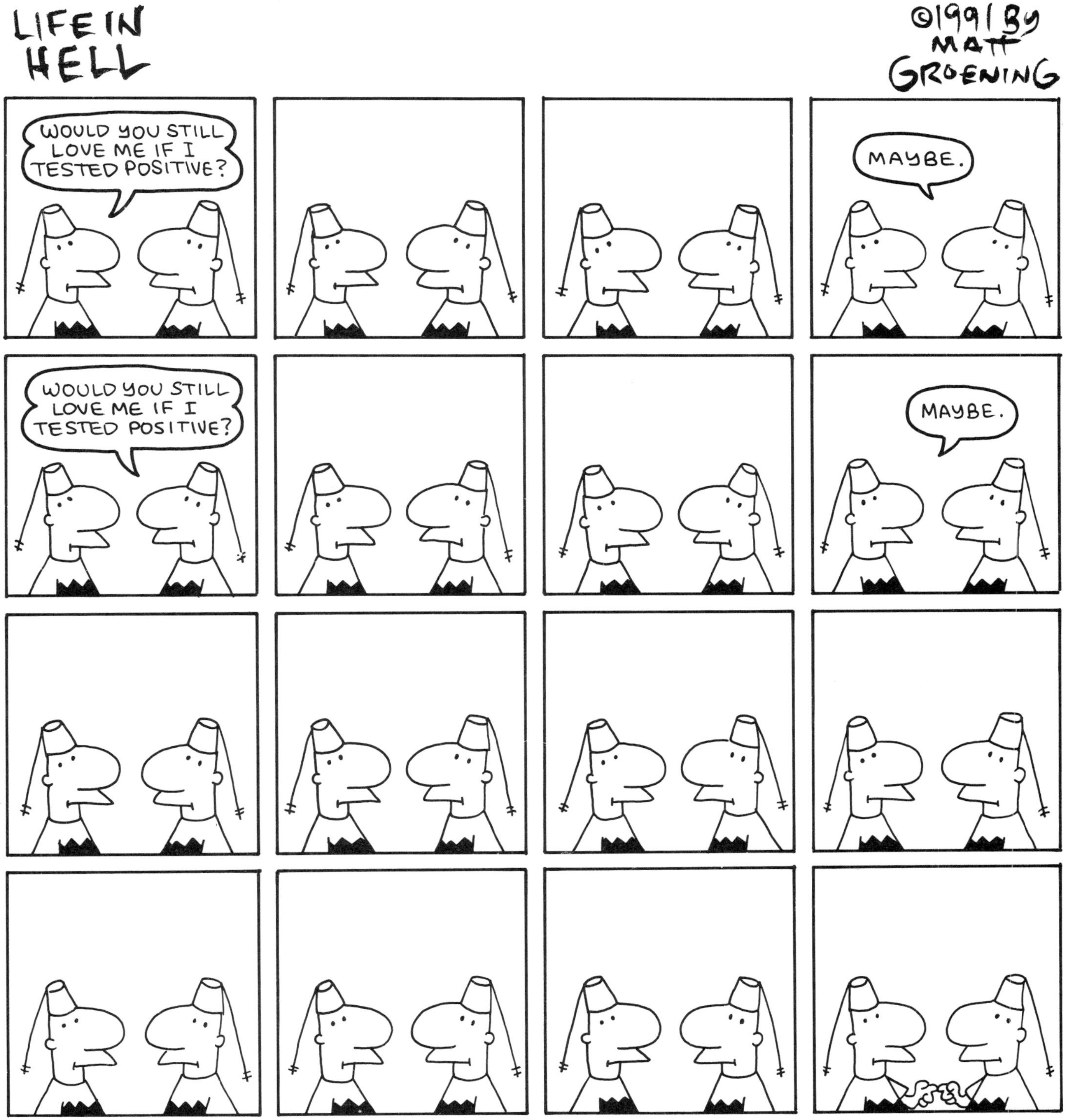
LIFE IN HELL
©1991 BY MATT GROENING
WOULD YOU STILL LOVE ME IF I TESTED POSITIVE?
MAYBE.
WOULD YOU STILL LOVE ME IF I TESTED POSITIVE?
MAYBE.

LIFE IN HELL

HOW TO OVERCOME STRESS AT WORK

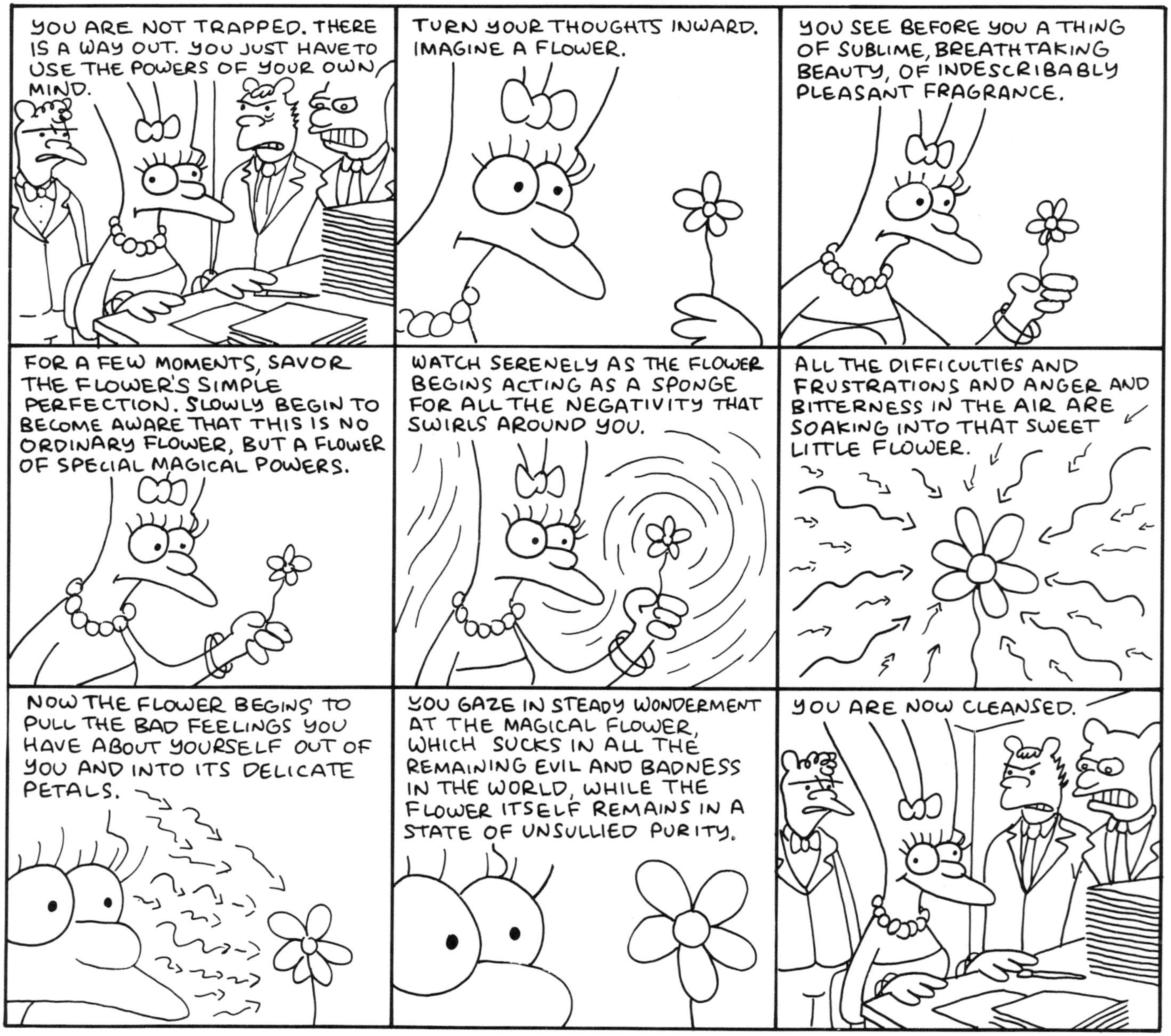
YOU ARE NOT TRAPPED. THERE IS A WAY OUT. YOU JUST HAVE TO USE THE POWERS OF YOUR OWN MIND.
TURN YOUR THOUGHTS INWARD. IMAGINE A FLOWER.
YOU SEE BEFORE YOU A THING OF SUBLIME, BREATHTAKING BEAUTY, OF INDESCRIBABLY PLEASANT FRAGRANCE.
FOR A FEW MOMENTS, SAVOR THE FLOWER'S SIMPLE PERFECTION. SLOWLY BEGIN TO BECOME AWARE THAT THIS IS NO ORDINARY FLOWER, BUT A FLOWER OF SPECIAL MAGICAL POWERS.
WATCH SERENELY AS THE FLOWER BEGINS ACTING AS A SPONGE FOR ALL THE NEGATIVITY THAT SWIRLS AROUND YOU.
ALL THE DIFFICULTIES AND FRUSTRATIONS AND ANGER AND BITTERNESS IN THE AIR ARE SOAKING INTO THAT SWEET LITTLE FLOWER.
NOW THE FLOWER BEGINS TO PULL THE BAD FEELINGS YOU HAVE ABOUT YOURSELF OUT OF YOU AND INTO ITS DELICATE PETALS.
YOU GAZE IN STEADY WONDERMENT AT THE MAGICAL FLOWER, WHICH SUCKS IN ALL THE REMAINING EVIL AND BADNESS IN THE WORLD, WHILE THE FLOWER ITSELF REMAINS IN A STATE OF UNSULLIED PURITY.
YOU ARE NOW CLEANSED.

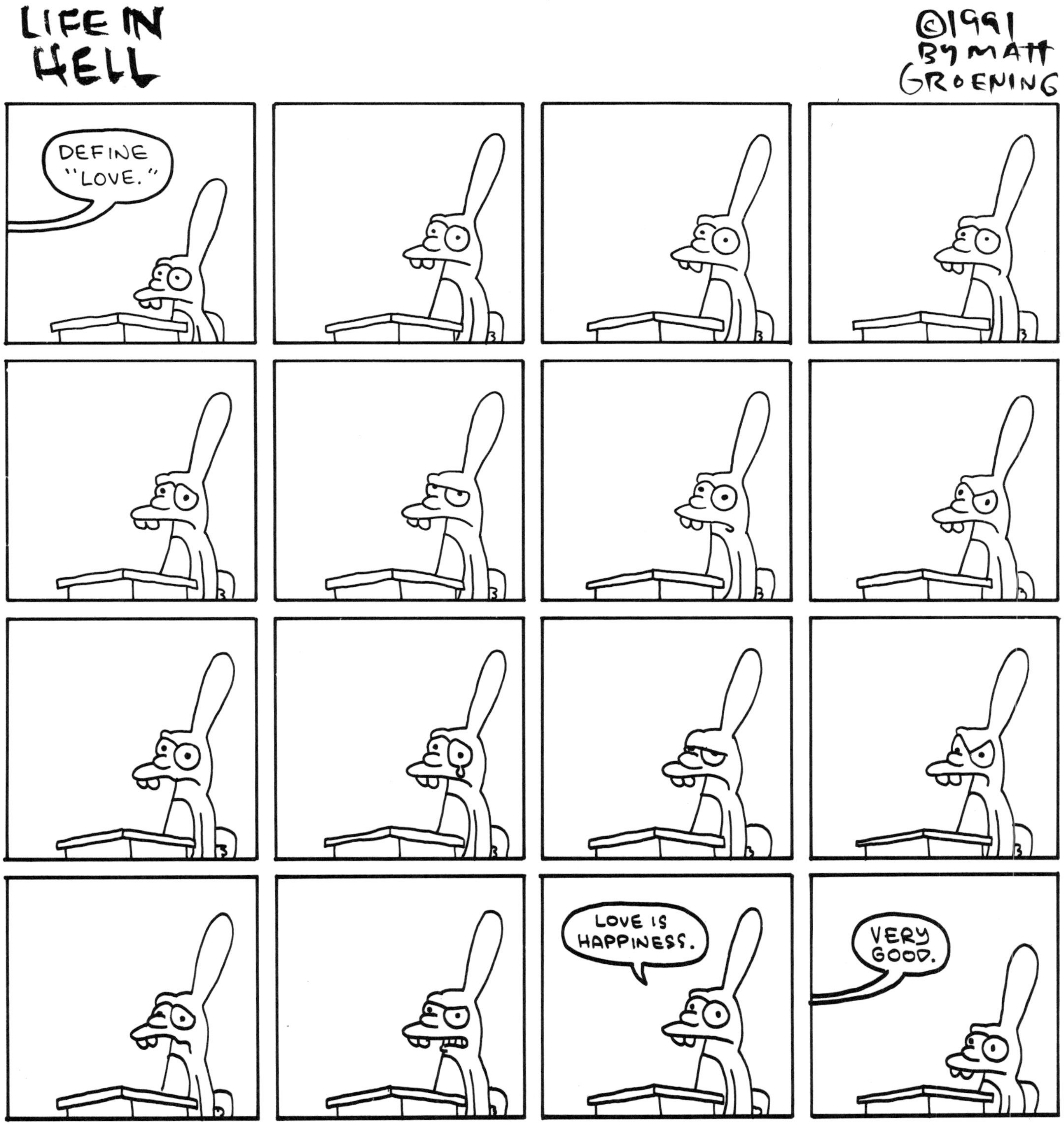
LIFE IN HELL
©1991 BY MATT GROENING
DEFINE "LOVE."
LOVE IS HAPPINESS.
VERY GOOD.

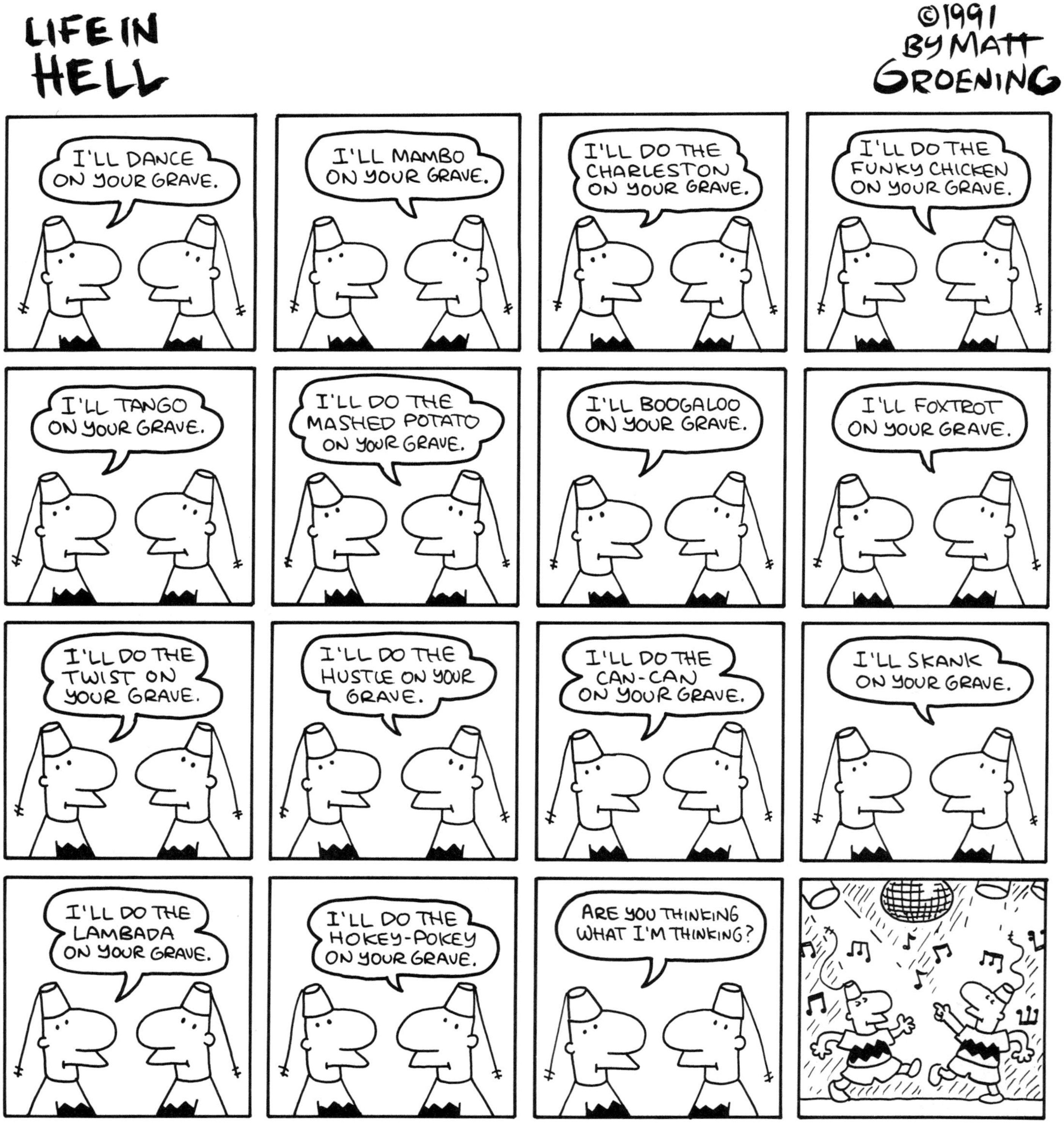
LIFE IN HELL
©1991 BY MATT GROENING
I'LL DANCE ON YOUR GRAVE.
I'LL MAMBO ON YOUR GRAVE.
I'LL DO THE CHARLESTON ON YOUR GRAVE.
I'LL DO THE FUNKY CHICKEN ON YOUR GRAVE.
I'LL TANGO ON YOUR GRAVE.
I'LL DO THE MASHED POTATO ON YOUR GRAVE.
I'LL BOOGALOO ON YOUR GRAVE.
I'LL FOXTROT ON YOUR GRAVE.
I'LL DO THE TWIST ON YOUR GRAVE.
I'LL DO THE HUSTLE ON YOUR GRAVE.
I'LL DO THE CAN-CAN ON YOUR GRAVE.
I'LL SKANK ON YOUR GRAVE.
I'LL DO THE LAMBADA ON YOUR GRAVE.
I'LL DO THE HOKEY-POKEY ON YOUR GRAVE.
ARE YOU THINKING WHAT I'M THINKING?

LIFE IN HELL

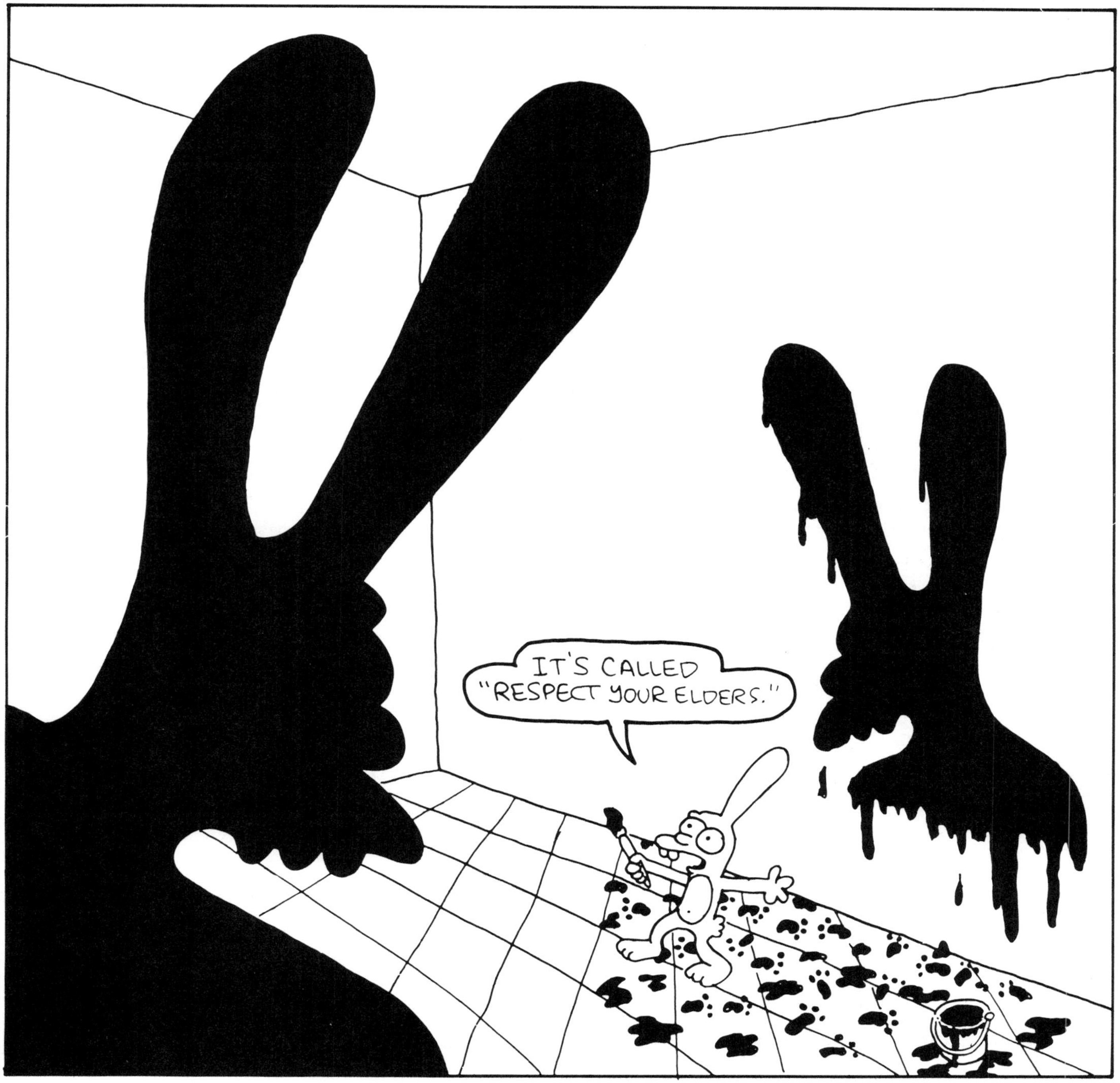
IT'S CALLED "RESPECT YOUR ELDERS."

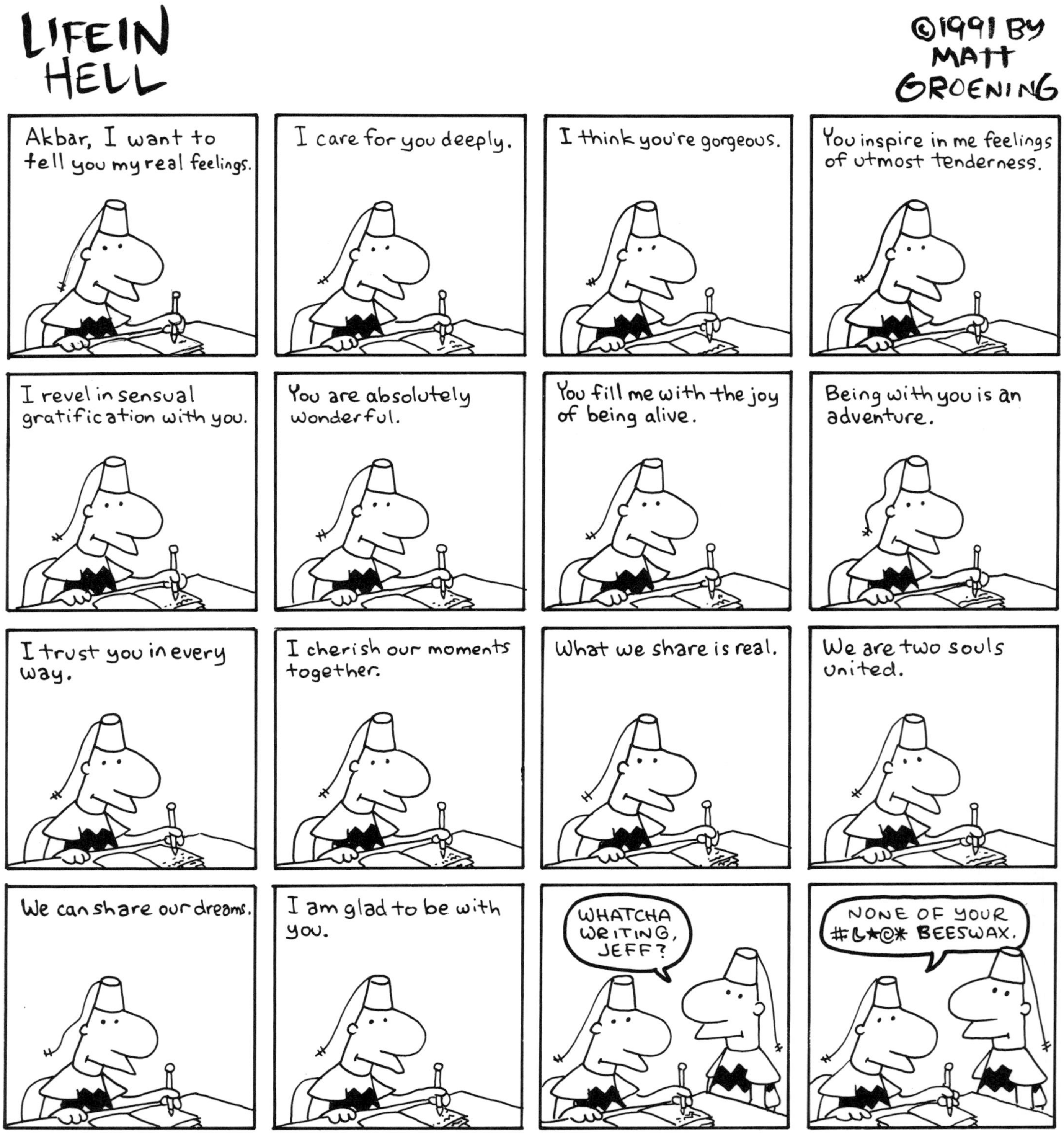
LIFE IN HELL
©1991 BY MATT GROENING
Akbar, I want to tell you my real feelings.
I care for you deeply.
I think you're gorgeous.
You inspire in me feelings of utmost tenderness.
I revel in sensual gratification with you.
You are absolutely wonderful.
You fill me with the joy of being alive.
Being with you is an adventure.
I trust you in every way.
I cherish our moments together.
What we share is real.
We are two souls united.
We can share our dreams.
I am glad to be with you.
WHATCHA WRITING, JEFF?
NONE OF YOUR #&*@* BEESWAX.

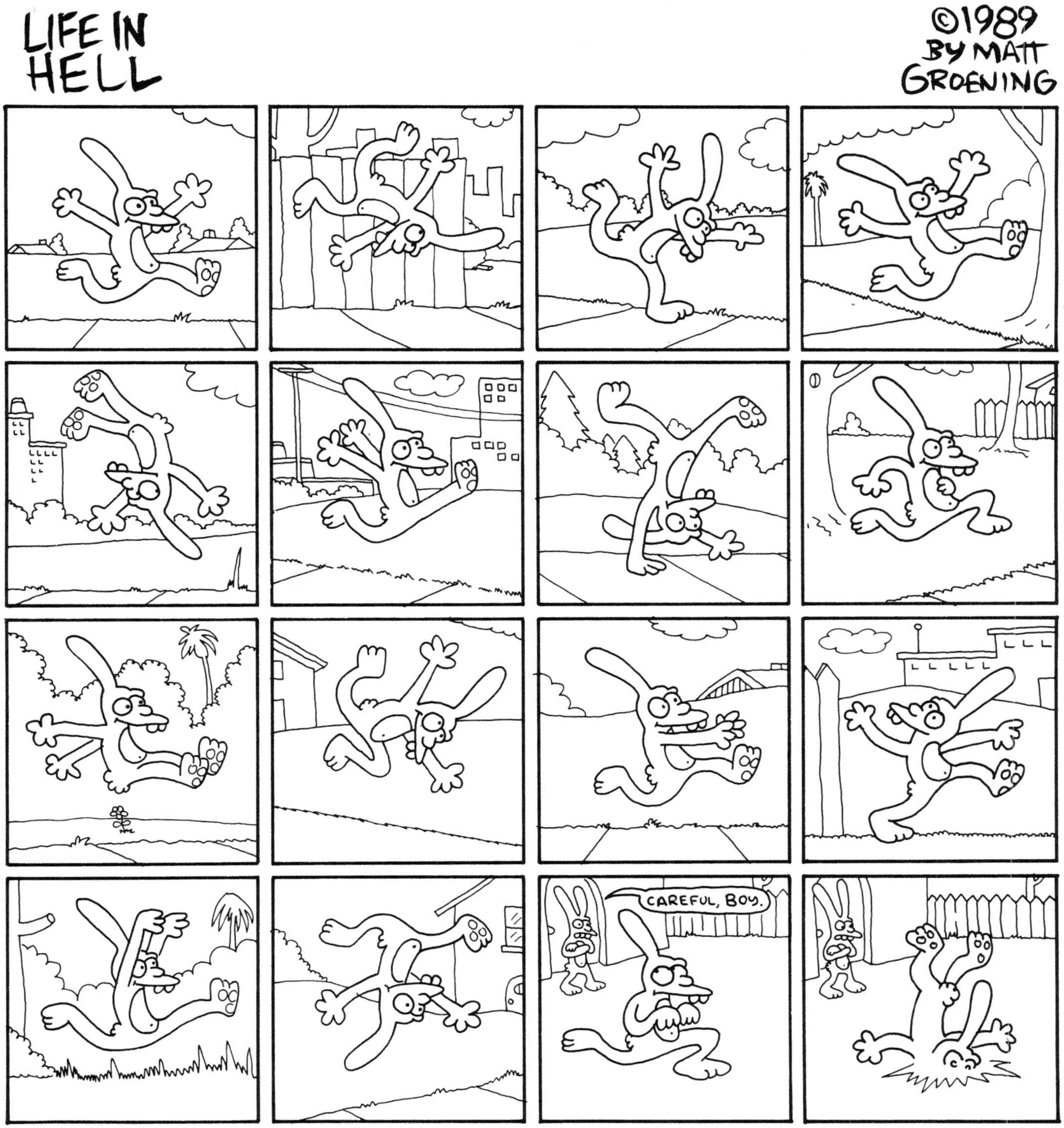
LIFE IN HELL
©1989 BY MATT GROENING
CAREFUL, BOY.

LIFE IN HELL

CALLING ALL CAFFEINE-ADDICTED MANIC-DEPRESSIVE CREATIVE TYPES!
GET OUT OF YOUR RATTY LITTLE APARTMENT AND LOITER SULLENLY AT

Akbar & Jeff's COFFEE HUT

FORMERLY AKBAR & JEFF'S FROZEN YOGURT HUT

OLDSTER BEATNIK SENIOR CITIZENS WELCOME IF YOU PROMISE NOT TO TELL US STORIES

"SERVING THE ALIENATED YOUNG RECOVERING ALCOHOLIC COMMUNITY SINCE 1990"

5% DISCOUNT IF YOU ARE ATTIRED SOLELY IN BLACK AND ARE WEARING SUNGLASSES AFTER DARK

• NO SHOES
• NO SHIRT
• NO NUKES

SCHEDULE

Mondays
ATONAL HOOTENANNY NITE If you like the sounds of industrial grinders you won't want to miss these young pioneers. A solemn time is guaranteed for all.

Wednesdays
TREASURES OF FRENCH SILENT AVANT-GARDE CINEMA The finest in scratchy 16mm 5th-generation duped prints will be shown on the far wall above the communal mural.

Thursdays
GIRLFRIENDS OF BITTER UNRECOGNIZED GENIUSES SUPPORT GROUP MEETING

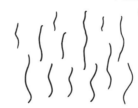

I SURVIVED OPEN MIKE POETRY NITE AT AKBAR & JEFF'S COFFEE HUT

SOUVENIR MUGS $5 WITH PURCHASE OF LARGE BEVERAGE AND PASTRY PLATTER

Fridays
MYSTERY CELEBRITY NITE Each week we present a reading by another legendary award-winning 1950s-era beat misogynist poet

Saturdays
PERFORMANCE ART NITE The management cautions you not to eat any substance thrown, thrusted, or proffered by the performers, no matter how edible-looking.

Sundays
OPEN MIKE POETRY NITE The action is nonstop in this literary free-for-all. Bring your poems, lyrics, manifestoes, dream journals, suicide notes -- and let the fun begin!

VISIT OUR POETRY BOOKSTORE ON THE PREMISES IN THE NOOK IN THE FAR CORNER! SPECIAL GET-ACQUAINTED SALE! ALL BOOKS ON SALE 10¢ A DOZEN! NO RETURNS.

"THE MANAGEMENT CANNOT ACCEPT RESPONSIBILITY FOR SERVING YOU REGULAR WHEN YOU ORDERED DECAF."

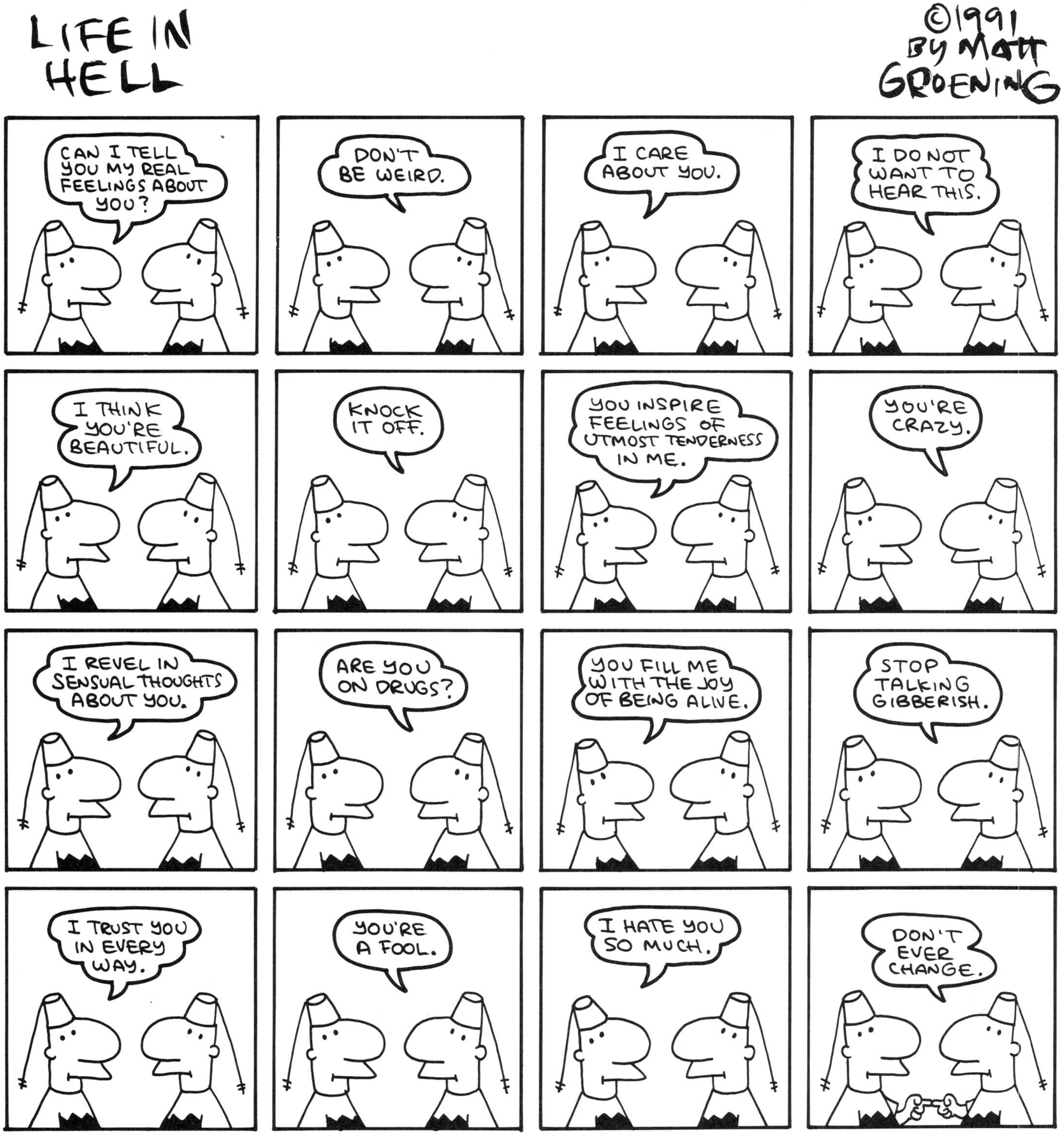
LIFE IN HELL
©1991 BY MATT GROENING
CAN I TELL YOU MY REAL FEELINGS ABOUT YOU?
DON'T BE WEIRD.
I CARE ABOUT YOU.
I DO NOT WANT TO HEAR THIS.
I THINK YOU'RE BEAUTIFUL.
KNOCK IT OFF.
YOU INSPIRE FEELINGS OF UTMOST TENDERNESS IN ME.
YOU'RE CRAZY.
I REVEL IN SENSUAL THOUGHTS ABOUT YOU.
ARE YOU ON DRUGS?
YOU FILL ME WITH THE JOY OF BEING ALIVE.
STOP TALKING GIBBERISH.
I TRUST YOU IN EVERY WAY.
YOU'RE A FOOL.
I HATE YOU SO MUCH.
DON'T EVER CHANGE.

LIFE IN HELL

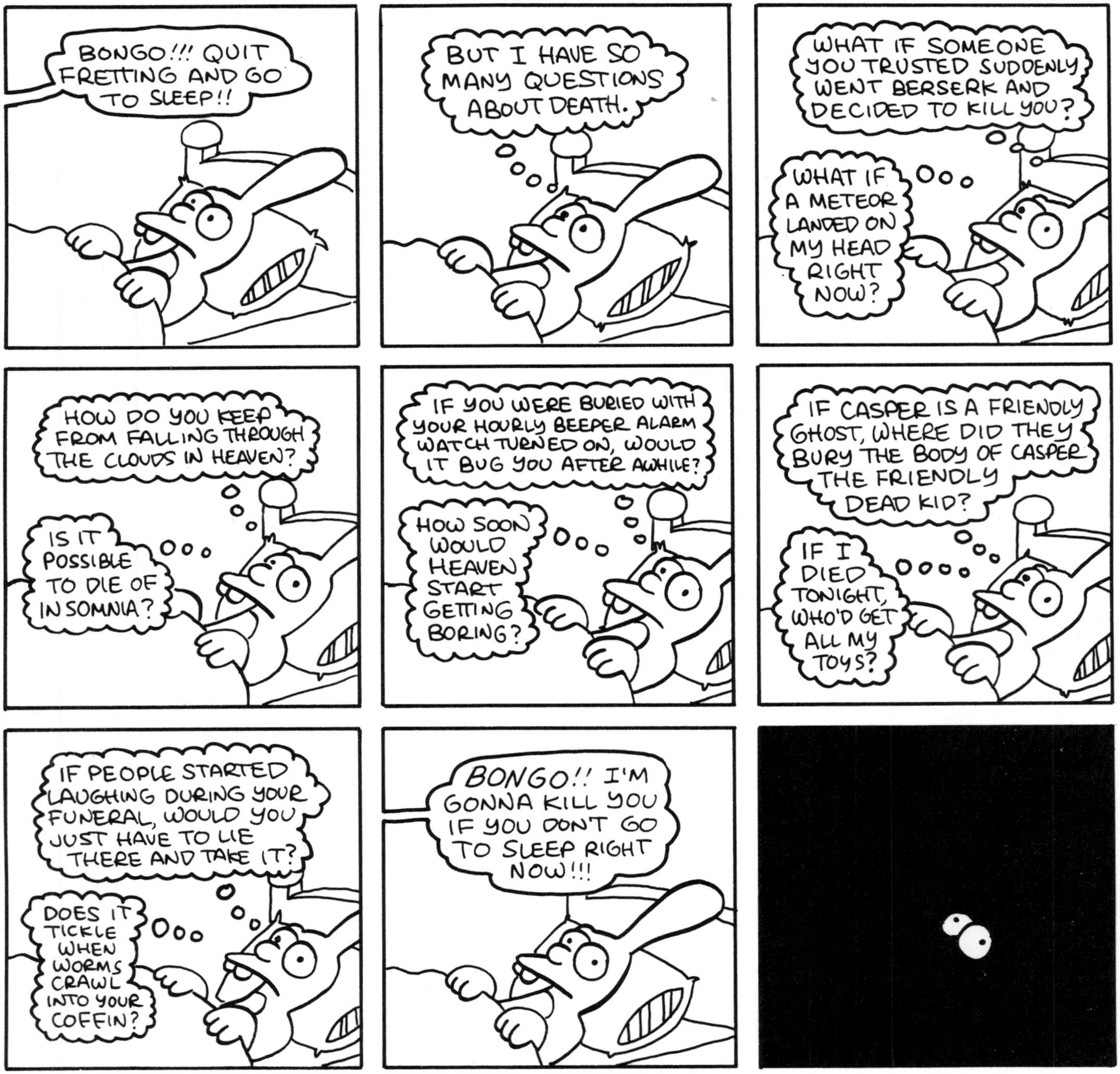
BONGO!!! QUIT FRETTING AND GO TO SLEEP!!
BUT I HAVE SO MANY QUESTIONS ABOUT DEATH.
WHAT IF SOMEONE YOU TRUSTED SUDDENLY WENT BERSERK AND DECIDED TO KILL YOU?
WHAT IF A METEOR LANDED ON MY HEAD RIGHT NOW?
HOW DO YOU KEEP FROM FALLING THROUGH THE CLOUDS IN HEAVEN?
IS IT POSSIBLE TO DIE OF INSOMNIA?
IF YOU WERE BURIED WITH YOUR HOURLY BEEPER ALARM WATCH TURNED ON, WOULD IT BUG YOU AFTER AWHILE?
HOW SOON WOULD HEAVEN START GETTING BORING?
IF CASPER IS A FRIENDLY GHOST, WHERE DID THEY BURY THE BODY OF CASPER THE FRIENDLY DEAD KID?
IF I DIED TONIGHT, WHO'D GET ALL MY TOYS?
IF PEOPLE STARTED LAUGHING DURING YOUR FUNERAL, WOULD YOU JUST HAVE TO LIE THERE AND TAKE IT?
DOES IT TICKLE WHEN WORMS CRAWL INTO YOUR COFFIN?
BONGO!! I'M GONNA KILL YOU IF YOU DON'T GO TO SLEEP RIGHT NOW!!!